Longeing and Long Lining
THE ENGLISH AND WESTERN HORSE:
A Total Program

ALSO BY CHERRY HILL

101 Longeing and Long Lining Exercises, English and Western
Beginning English Exercises
Intermediate English Exercises
Advanced English Exercises
Beginning Western Exercises
Intermediate Western Exercises
Advanced Western Exercises
Horse for Sale
Maximum Hoof Power (with Richard Klimesh)
101 Arena Exercises
Horsekeeping on a Small Acreage
Becoming an Effective Rider
The Formative Years
Making Not Breaking
From the Center of the Ring
Your Pony, Your Horse
Horse Handling and Grooming
Horse Health Care
Horseowner's Guide to Lameness (with Dr. Ted S. Stashak)

Longeing and Long Lining
THE ENGLISH AND WESTERN HORSE:
A Total Program

Cherry Hill

Photographs by **Richard Klimesh**

Howell Book House

New York

The information given in this book is provided for the purpose of education and to give as complete a picture as possible. The reader, even if experienced in the handling of horses, should exercise extreme care in all circumstances.

Howell Book House
A Simon & Schuster Macmillan Company
1633 Broadway
New York, NY 10019

Macmillan Publishing books may be purchased for business or sales promotional use. For information please write: Special Markets Department, Macmillan Publishing USA, 1633 Broadway, New York, NY

MACMILLAN is a registered trademark of Macmillan, Inc.

Library of Congress Cataloging information available upon request.

ISBN 0-87605-080-1

Manufactured in the United States of America

10–9–8–7–6–5–4–3–2–1

Book Design: Rachael McBrearty—Madhouse Studios
Cover Design: Michele Laseau

Contents

Acknowledgments

THANKS TO:

Richard Klimesh, photographer, for his keen interest in the project and his unique perspective while shooting.

Ariat International for safe, comfortable English and Western boots.

Top Tack, Inc. for specialized, innovative, high-quality tack for longeing and ground driving.

Topline Horse Gear for a wide variety of tack for ground training.

Les Vogt's Equiline for snaffle bits for the Western horse.

Pro Equine Division of Farnam for protective leg boots.

THANKS TO MY COOPERATIVE EQUINE MODELS:

Doctor Zip
Ben Dickens
Aria
Seeker
Drifter's Eclipse
Poco Pine Pete

Preface

As I work with a horse, my primary goal is to gain his trust and respect. With that established, we can develop a specialized system of communication that not only *allows* us to work together but actually *invites* us to interact. We both look forward to the sessions. The horse meets me at the gate. He's willing and interested. I am inspired and motivated by the progress and spirit of the horse and can't wait to get to the barn. In this way, we become enthusiastic working partners. That is my long-term goal: a solid partnership where we can count on each other and take care of each other.

Although I want the horse to bond with me and respond to me, I do not want him to be a pet or depend on me to direct his every step. I want him to be a self-confident animal. After all, it is the spirit of the horse that has attracted me. Continual prodding and nagging have no place. That would be too disrespectful of the horse and it would take the joy out of horse training for me.

In order to safely and effectively work together, I must learn something about the horse and the horse must learn something about me. The best way to accomplish this is through consistent daily handling. Every day, I approach every horse encounter as training. The way the horse and I interact when I feed, clean the pen or stall, halter, and lead, or turn the horse out for exercise are just as important as the lessons in the training pen. The horse is always learning. And so am I. Trainers have to be life-long learners.

When it comes time for what is usually considered "formal" training—in-hand maneuvers, longeing, ground driving, and riding—the horse that has become a partner will take new lessons willingly.

Nowhere can you better prepare a horse for the requirements of riding than in a comprehensive ground-training program. And even after a horse is a very experienced riding horse, longeing and long lining provide an excellent means for monitoring progress, giving a horse a tune-up, or introducing new concepts.

Thorough ground training makes a horse safer, more confident, and more comfortable to ride. That's why I've written this book, and its companion volume, *101 Longeing and Long Lining Exercises: English and Western.*

Here I discuss the total program. Besides explaining ground-training philosophies and procedures, I cover the "behind the scenes" concepts and ideas that will help you formulate your own personalized training program. By knowing "why," you will be able to tailor a program to suit both you and your horse. To illustrate the stages of groundwork, I have included photographs of horses of different sexes, ages, and breeds in different stages of training. In many instances, the photos depict the first lesson for a horse in a particular phase.

I encourage you to first become thoroughly familiar with the total program. Then, you can tailor your longeing and long lining progression to suit your facilities, your goals, your horse's characteristics, and your time schedule. If you don't have a round pen, you'll want to incorporate free longeing techniques in your first work on a longe line. If you are not experienced enough for or your goals don't require the use of side reins, you might choose to develop contact with long lining. All along the way, you will make choices as you formulate your own personal training program.

In *101 Longeing and Long Lining Exercises: English and Western,* I compiled my favorite ground-training exercises. You can use the exercise book as a workbook to plan your daily sessions with each horse as well as to set long-term goals. With each exercise, I've included how-to diagrams and step-by-step instructions.

It is my hope that these two books inspire you and give you direction so you can develop a solid, working relationship with your horse.

LONGEING IS MORE THAN TROTTING IN A CIRCLE

First, is it *longeing, lungeing, longing,* or *lounging* and what does it mean? Derived from the French *allonge,* which means "extension," *longe* is the most correct English variation. I choose to use *longe* (*longeing*) so as to differentiate it from the word *lunge,* which is a sudden thrust, or plunge forward, something I associate more with fencing than working a horse around me in a circle. The confusion comes in that *longe* is pronounced the same as *lunge. Longing* and *lounging,* the other two Americanized versions of the word appear regionally in speech, but not too often in writing. Although you may *wish* your horse were trained, *longing* will not make it so. And when you are working a couch potato horse, he might try to convince you it is supposed to be *lounging,* but you must let him know that is not what you have in mind!

Longeing is often the transition training between in-hand work and riding. It offers the means to introduce the horse to many of the requirements and sensations associated with riding. That's why longeing should always encourage good movement, a good attitude, and good manners.

Longeing Pros and Cons

Longeing is much more than a horse trotting in a circle. It refers to a trainer working a horse in a circle at various gaits, either free in a round pen or on a line that is 30 to 35 feet long. Longeing is a specific, controlled lesson progression in a horse's ground-training program, *not* a random activity where the horse races around the pen, unbalanced and out of control.

Although longeing is generally thought of as a means to either train a young horse or warm up an experienced horse before a ride, the benefits of and uses for longeing are so varied that it should be a part of the training and exercise program of all horses.

Long lining, which is also called ground driving, long reining, and double longeing, is working the horse on two lines, one attached to each side of the longeing cavesson or bit. Since it comes later in the horse's training progression, it is covered toward the end of the book.

Minimize Stress

Because longeing is repetitive movement, it can stress the horse's limbs. It is best to wait until a horse is at least two years old before you start his longeing training in earnest. Although it is beneficial to give a yearling a few lessons in a round pen to teach him to face you or stop when commanded, the real longeing program should not begin until 24 months of age.

Working a horse of any age in a repetitious circle can stress the legs from the continuous canting, and may result in lameness. Following these recommendations can minimize the stress to the limbs:

Be sure the footing is not slippery.

Don't work a horse in excessively deep footing. Two to four inches is optimum.

Work the horse in a circle 66 feet in diameter or larger (that means a 33-foot longe line used full length).

Only walk and trot horses younger than two years of age.

With a two-year-old, use cantering only to teach the horse the transition from trot to canter. Don't require the young horse to canter for long periods of time. Cantering heavily loads the leading foreleg and should be avoided as a means of conditioning until all the horse's epiphyses have closed at 24 months of age.

If you use longeing too often or too long, it can bore both you and your horse. To prevent boredom with longeing, teach your horse a variety of longeing skills, ask your horse for many transitions, work him on circles of varying sizes, and hold the session in various places—the round pen, arena, and pasture.

As you longe your horse, focus on developing and maintaining contact with the longe line, shaping the horse with whip position and body language, and regulating impulsion with a variety of voice commands.

Other Uses for Longeing

The Longe Lesson

Once a horse is solidly trained on the longe line, he can be used to teach a rider seat and position while an instructor guides the horse from the ground. The horse can work without interference from the rider's hands. Often the main objective of longe lessons is to teach the rider to establish a supple, secure seat that follows the

movements of the horse. Longe lessons include exercises that help you find your seat bones, keep your weight evenly distributed on both seat bones at all times, deepen your seat, relax your lower back and shoulders, improve your posture and breathing, stretch your muscles, strengthen your abdominal muscles, align your body (notably your spine), and discover the effect your seat alone can have on the horse.

A longe-lesson horse must be even-tempered, focused, very experienced at longeing, comfortable with all the tack necessary for the longe lesson—especially side reins—and obedient to voice commands, especially "*Whoa*" (Photo 1.1). A horse who has elastic movement and good

1.1 *Your instructor and a well-trained longe horse are valuable mentors who can help you develop a secure, balanced, and independent seat.*

THE BENEFITS OF LONGEING

Develops obedience to voice commands and body language.

Establishes the foundation for long driving.

Is a progressive step in the horse's education. Makes the transition from in-hand work to mounted work logical and systematic.

Develops added confidence and familiarity between horse and trainer; sets the stage for upcoming learning. Adds a margin of safety for mounted work.

Allows for familiarity with tack, such as carrying an "inert" snaffle.

Introduces movement principles: balance, rhythm, vertical and lateral flexion, gait extension, and collection without interference from a rider.

Is helpful for correcting bad habits such as impure gaits, head tossing, or spooking.

Teaches a horse to work in certain confines.

Allows the horse to develop physically: left/right balance, suppleness, strength of back and loin, tendon and ligament durability without the weight of a rider.

Is valuable for rehabilitation after illness, injury, or pregnancy/lactation; can gain greater exercise effect than with hand walking, yet is safer than turn-out.

Is good for warm-up and cool-down for any riding horse.

Allows the trainer to observe the horse while the horse is moving, which provides a chance to assess ability, soundness, quality of movement, gait purity, way of going, way of approaching obstacles, etc.

Allows the trainer to keep a horse in work when the trainer is pregnant, has a temporary riding impairment, or a schedule crunch.

Provides an exercise alternative for indoor work when the outside footing is too treacherous for riding.

Provides an exercise alternative for use in unfenced areas such as on show grounds.

Can be used for rider longe lessons and self-longe lessons.

Can be used to introduce cavalletti work and jumping.

Can be used to introduce and hone obstacle work.

Is a requirement of the Longe Line Class in horse shows.

SOME LONGEING CAUTIONS

Common longe lines are 25 feet long, so horses often are worked on circles smaller than 50 feet in diameter. The torque on limb structures during small circle work can be damaging, especially if at speed or if repeated often.

Horses are often not trained properly and see longeing as a time to play, race around, and hurt themselves; interference and tendon strain are the most common injuries.

Horses can learn bad habits of carriage such as hollow back, high head, and short, quick stride when improperly longed.

Horses can learn bad habits related to improperly applied tack such as behind the bit, a dropped poll, bucking, rearing.

Longeing, if improperly approached or overused, can bore a horse and make him sour about work in general.

Longeing can easily turn into a counter-productive activity. If the lessons are random or tack is used improperly, longeing can result in a horse:

• Becoming stiffer rather than more supple.

• Becoming heavy on the forehand rather than more balanced.

• Developing a hollow topline rather than a rounded one.

• Developing short, choppy movement rather than long, flowing movement.

Longeing can be overused. It might be necessary, for safety reasons, to longe a particularly spirited horse before riding. If it is always needed to tire a horse, it may become a time-consuming dependency.

Longeing might not be appropriate training for a roping prospect. If a horse receives a great deal of longeing training, when the time comes for roping, his association with a long line/rope might cause him to circle the calf or steer instead of holding the rope stretched.

impulsion will better teach the student how to follow movement.

It is most helpful if the longe-lesson pilot is your regular riding instructor, but if you have a friend who is very competent and comfortable longeing, you can use him or her as well. The lesson can be held wherever the horse is customarily worked.

During lessons, your instructor gives you feedback that will help you correlate

OBSERVE AND EVALUATE MOVEMENT

Use your vantage point at the center of the longeing circle to observe and evaluate the following:

ACTION The style of the movement—including joint flexion, stride length, and suspension—as viewed from the side as the horse works the large circle.

ASYMMETRY A difference between pairs of body parts or an alteration in the synchronization of a gait. When a horse is performing asymmetrically, he is often said to be "off"; noted as a difference in swing, landing, or weight-bearing of one of the limbs.

BALANCE The harmonious, precise, co-ordinated form of a horse's movement as reflected by equal distribution of weight from left to right and an appropriate amount of weight carried by the hindquarters. Balance is closely tied in with straightness; a balanced horse travels "straight," an unbalanced horse overbent or counterflexed.

BREAKOVER The moment between the stance and swing phases as the heel lifts and the hoof pivots over the toe. Breakover will be altered in deep or wet footing and when hoof is out of balance.

CADENCE See Rhythm.

COLLECTION A shortening of stride within a gait, without a decrease in tempo. It is brought about by a shift of the center of gravity rearward and is usually accompanied by an overall body elevation and an increase in joint flexion.

DIRECTNESS Trueness of travel, the straightness of the line in which the hoof (limb) is carried forward; difficult to see on the longeing circle unless the gait defect (winging, paddling) is very exaggerated.

EVENNESS Balance, symmetry, and synchronization of the steps within a gait in terms of weight-bearing and timing. True two-beat trot, three-beat canter/lope, four-beat, flat-footed walk, etc. are required in the show ring. No mixed gaits; observe tendencies and nip them in the bud.

EXTENSION A lengthening of stride within a gait, without an increase in tempo, brought about by a driving force from behind and a reaching in front. It is usually accompanied by a horizontal floating called *suspension*. On a large circle or a straightaway, the gaits can be lengthened, but true extension will probably have to wait until mounted work.

GAIT An orderly footfall pattern such as the walk, trot, canter (see Evenness).

HEIGHT The degree of elevation of arc of the stride as viewed from the side; this will be altered by the horse's excitement and energy level and the footing.

IMPULSION Thrust, or the manner in which the horse's weight is settled and released from the supporting structures of the limb in the act of carrying the horse forward. It is also the forward motion that is necessary

OBSERVE AND EVALUATE MOVEMENT (CONTINUED)

for every movement and a solution to many problems.

OVERTRACK "Tracking up"; the horse's hind feet step on or ahead of the front prints.

POWER Propelling, balancing (and sometimes pulling) forces originating primarily in the hindquarters.

RAPIDITY Promptness, quickness; the time consumed in taking a single stride. Usually rapidity is not desired and develops into problems with gait purity and balance; however, lazy, sloppy movement is not desirable either.

REGULARITY The cadence, the rhythmical precision with which each stride is taken in turn; the piston-like precision of horses with great impulsion and timing.

RELAXATION Absence of excess muscular tension. It begins with mental relaxation and familiarity with the task at hand and is necessary for productive work. Evident as lowered frame, swinging tail, soft snorting or blowing, etc.

RHYTHM The cadence of the footfall within a gait, taking into account timing (number of beats) and accent.

STEP A single beat of a gait. A step may involve one or more limbs. In the walk, there are four individual steps. In the trot, there are two steps, both involving two limbs.

STIFFNESS Inability (because of pain or lack of condition) or unwillingness (bad attitude) to flex and extend the muscles or joints; usually evident as hollow back, hindquarters behind the action, high head, short strides.

STRAIGHTNESS The hind feet traveling in the path of the front feet, even when on a circle. The inner hind leg, as it comes forward, must move slightly toward the outside of the longe circle, thereby coming under the center of gravity (see Balance).

STRIDE, LENGTH OF The distance from the point of breaking over to the point of next contact with the ground of the same hoof; also a full sequence of steps in a particular gait.

SUPPLENESS Flexibility; the ability to flex and bend in circular movements without excess tension.

SUSPENSION The horizontal floating that occurs when a limb is extended and the body continues moving forward; also refers to the moment at the canter and gallop when all limbs are flexed or curled up, reorganizing for the next stride.

TEMPO The rate of movement; the rate of stride repetition. A faster tempo results in more strides per minute. The tempo should remain constant within a gait, no matter whether it is regular, collected, or extended; only the stride length should change.

the correct seat position with the way it feels. In addition, you are likely to find some of the many incorrect variations to rider position, how they feel, and how to correct them. During your longe lessons, you should make a mental checklist of the sensations and identify which are coupled with the correct position and which need correction.

It takes six months to one year of concentrated effort to develop a good seat or to correct a faulty one. Longe lessons for the rider are very beneficial to this end. They help you find balance on a moving horse, and they allow you to concentrate on eliminating imbalances or crooked body positions. The seat must be supple, upright, and forward, yet deep and independent from the other aids. Longe lessons also provide a good opportunity for you to develop proper leg contact and position, which is directly related to the development of the seat. The reason an instructor-controlled longe lesson is so valuable is that you can concentrate totally on your position because you do not have to guide the horse.

Wear an approved protective helmet. Outfit the English saddle with a bucking strap that attaches to the D-rings on either side of the pommel. You can grab the bucking strap if you lose your balance. Western saddles have a horn and swells that you can grab. Don't wear spurs or carry a whip.

The lesson horse should be longed first, the side reins adjusted, and the horse warmed up until his back is relaxed and rounded and his gaits are rhythmic and even. While the instructor is warming up the horse, you should do some simple stretching exercises as preparation.

The Self-Longe Lesson

There is no substitute for a good instructor. But between lessons, giving yourself a longe lesson may help you strengthen and correct your seat and position. In some instances, a very trustworthy horse and an experienced rider can work together on automatic pilot so that the rider can develop balance, rhythm, and harmony (Photo 1.2). In a self-longe lesson, you will have to initiate gait transitions, but should not have to do more.

Therefore, for self-longe lessons, a very steady, well-schooled horse is necessary. The horse must be sound and trustworthy. His rhythm must be consistent, with no increase or decrease within or between gaits unless those changes are called for. He must accept fairly snug contact with the side reins because they will help to keep him organized. He should be physically able and mentally willing to

1.2 *If you are an experienced rider, and have access to a round pen and a very trustworthy horse, you can give yourself a longe lesson. The horse continues on automatic pilot while you deepen your seat, develop a secure leg, and become less dependent on the reins.*

stand quietly at a halt with the side reins attached. A horse who backs, throws his head, or swerves the hindquarters instead of standing at a square halt is not reliable enough for use in a self-longe lesson.

The horse must be relatively balanced from side to side as well as from front to rear so that he performs without falling on the forehand, leaning on the side reins, or drifting in or out of the circle. The self-longe horse must be able and willing to perform the gaits in a quiet rhythm as well as at a more active pace as the rider's development dictates. It is not necessary for the self-longe horse to be a spectacular or elegant mover. As long as his rhythm and balance are relatively steady and he works with relaxation, he will allow the rider to work on the same.

The self-longe lesson must be held in a round pen. Twenty meters in diameter (66 feet across) is best because it will allow the horse to bend evenly. Footing in the pen should be dry and not excessively deep or hard. The horse is outfitted with an English or Western saddle. It is best to remove the stirrups. The bridle reins can remain attached and be fixed safely out of the way, where the rider can grab them in an emergency. Elastic side reins are attached from the bit to the customary place on the saddle for that horse. (See Chapter 5, "Tack Tactics.") The side reins should be adjusted evenly and with a contact that is suitable for the horse. You should wear a protective helmet.

It might be necessary to longe the horse first to take off the edge before you mount. In any event, for the first self-lesson or so, it would be best to have a competent person on hand to start the horse, if necessary, and watch to be sure the horse is suitable for such work.

The Longe Line Class

The Longe Line Class is a relatively new horse show class introduced by some breed associations in the 1990s. It is primarily a class for yearlings or two-year-olds to exhibit their natural movement, attitude, and talent on the longe line. The rules vary between associations but generally the horse is shown in a halter and on a 30-foot longe line. The exhibitor has 1-1/2 minutes to show the horse at the walk, trot, and lope in each direction, but it is not mandatory that the horses perform all three gaits in each direction. After the individual longe work,

the horse's conformation is evaluated. The judging is usually 70 percent on the movement while longeing and 30 percent on conformation. The movement of the horse should be natural with good movement and manners. If the horse plays on the line, it is not to be counted against him. If a horse displays excessive running, bucking, tail wringing, or ear pinning, the penalty is up to the judge's discretion.

Safe Facilities

Training facilities—especially those used for longeing and long lining—need to be strong and safe. A horse's unpredictability and power should never be underestimated.

While you are tacking up your horse, he will be tied to a hitching post, rail, tie ring, or in crossties. If you tie him to a post, it should be with a quick-release knot and at a level at or above his withers.

If he's tied to a rail, it must be very stout. If a horse just once pulls off a rail or breaks it and panics with the rail following, he will be very frightened and could be dangerous for a very long time whenever he is tied.

If you tack up in crossties, be sure they are located in a safe, uncluttered area, are of the proper height, and are securely attached to the wall. All crossties should have a quick-release snap or knot.

The training pen and arena where you hold the longeing lessons must be entirely enclosed and must be of sturdy design and constructed of strong materials. Training a horse in an enclosure that has flimsy fences is just asking for trouble. The first time a horse is pressured, he might not only take out a section of the fence but also injure you and himself.

Round Pen

Many of the lessons are best performed in a small enclosure. For longeing and driving, a round pen is preferred to square or rectangular pens because there are no corners for the young horse to duck into for evasion (Photo 1.3). The optimum size is 66 feet in diameter, which is the equivalent of a 20-meter circle. The horse travels on a 33-foot longe line.

Smaller pens will allow you to work closer to your horse and could result in more control in some situations but more danger in others. Also, the smaller the pen,

1.3 *This round pen is 20 meters (66 feet) in diameter and has 6-foot-high sturdy rails. It's ideal for longeing and long lining and makes a good place to take first rides on an inexperienced horse.*

the more stress the horse's legs receive when he's working in circles.

What type of sides the pen has is very important. A breaking pen that is built solely for gentling fairly wild horses might be better if it has solid walls to ensure that the horse pays attention to you and to prevent the horse from climbing out of the pen. Walls are safer than rails in terms of horse leg injuries but can present quite a danger if you get pinned against a wall or need to exit the pen in a hurry.

Also, there comes a time when every horse must listen to you in spite of outside distractions. After all, the goal is to be able to handle the horse in a variety of situations, not just in the privacy of a solid-wall round pen. Also, solid-wall pens are more expensive to construct and maintain. That's why, in most situations, pens with rails are used.

A four- or five-rail round pen allows the young horse to see his environment. The training that takes place in an open-style pen will be more valuable when the horse's lessons are transferred to an arena or open area.

The round pen should have walls or rails high enough to discourage a horse from attempting to jump them. Six feet works for most breeds. If you choose to use rails, 8- or 10-inch boards that are at least 2 inches thick are recommended. Maximum length of the boards should be about 8 feet. Spanning a greater distance does not provide a secure enough barrier if a horse falls against the fence.

Posts 6 to 8 inches in diameter should be set deeply and at an angle so that the walls of the pen tip slightly outward (mine are at a 10-degree angle) to keep the horse from scraping saddles and tack on the rails. The angle will later accommodate your leg when you ride (Photo 1-4). The gate should be flush on the inside

with no protrusions of bolts, latches, or hinges.

Metal round pens put together from 10- or 12-foot-long panels may or may not be safe or strong enough for ground train-

1.4 *The boards are nailed on the inside of the posts, and the walls of the round pen angle outward at about 10 to 15 degrees. Both of these features protect horse and rider. The sand footing is held in place by railroad ties fitted between the posts.*

ing. Although they are portable and can be set up without digging fence posts, most metal panels are not tall enough for ground training. If you can find 6-foot tall panels that are stout enough and have small spaces between the rails and safe feet that won't trap a horse's legs, perhaps they could serve as a temporary option. The cost of these premium panels, however if you can find them—is quite a bit higher than that of building a wooden pen like the one illustrated here. (Also see *Horsekeeping on a Small Acreage* in Recommended Reading.)

The footing of a round pen should be well drained and provide cushion. Sand works well but depth is an important consideration. Four inches should provide the necessary cover for most activities. More might be too fatiguing to the horse's legs; less might not provide enough cushion. Placing the sand on well-drained native soil is the best. Fitting railroad ties between the bases of the posts will hold the sand in the round pen.

Once a horse has been taught to longe and drive in a round pen, you will want to hold some of his lessons in an arena where you can practice a wider variety of maneuvers.

Arena

The arena should be at least 66 feet by 132 feet, but 100 feet by 200 feet or larger will allow you to practice serpentines and more changes of direction (Photo 1.5).

The fence around the arena should be at least 6 feet tall and made from sturdy materials. Once a horse is trained, it is possible to longe him in an area that has low rails, such as a dressage ring, or in an open area. During the training phase, however, it is best to work in an enclosed area because it isn't uncommon for a young, frightened, or confused horse to bolt and get away from his trainer.

1.5 *This 100-foot by 200-foot arena makes an ideal place to longe and long line. Here the horse is being worked on a 35-foot line, so he is on a 70-foot circle.*

Footing

The ideal footing for training young horses is a surface similar to what they will be worked on as adults. If they are geared for arena competition, an arena with four inches of well-drained, cushiony surface material over a solid base will be fine for longeing, driving, and riding. More advanced lessons can be held in the open on turf with gently uneven terrain. Until the youngster gains some experience and conditioning, it is best to hold the training sessions in an enclosed level area that provides adequate cushion.

Footing is composed of the base, the surface material, and additives. The layer of material between the "earth" and the surface material is called the *base*. The functions of the base include acting as a protective layer between the earth and the surface material, giving stability to the arena floor, and carrying rainwater off the arena. The base might be naturally occurring material (such as decomposed granite) or added material (such as road base or fine gravel, topped with stone dust and clay). The base must contain no stones, and it needs to be packed or tamped as hard as concrete. The base layer must be thick enough to prevent material from the earth layer (such as stones) from working up to the surface material. A 4- to 6-inch base is usually sufficient for an arena that is used primarily for longe-ing, ground driving, and riding on the flat.

The base must be protected from damage caused by erosion, deep discing, and penetration from hooves. Regular maintenance should eliminate the potential for ruts forming along the rail.

The layer over the base is called the *cushion* or the *surface*. Often it is a mixture of materials. Depending on the base and use of the arena, the surface layer could be from 2 to 6 inches deep. The function of the surface material is to provide a cushioning effect. Three to four inches of surface footing seem to work well in many arenas.

Surface recipes vary widely and include mixtures of sand, silt, clay, topsoil, sawdust, and various artificial footings such as rubber.

Additives are soil conditioners and aerators designed to keep the surface material from packing or getting too dusty.

2

THE MASTER PLAN FOR TRAINER AND HORSE

As your work you horse on the longe line or long lines, you both will be developing skills and routines. Your progress will be enhanced if you outline the training program, set goals, make regular evaluations of your progress, and periodically modify your master plan.

Formulating the Training Plan

You have a variety of subjective and objective goals to accomplish during your horse's ground training. The work should be approached so the horse develops a confident, steady manner with a cooperative attitude and free, supple, forward movement characterized by a consistent rhythm. During the lessons, he should accept the bit, respond to the aids, work relatively straight and show "speed control": *extending* (moving on) and *collecting* (shortening) in his gaits. His frame should be allowed to develop naturally and progressively from the head up and nose out "kid frame" to a gradual rounding of the topline that leads to a collected advanced frame. Throughout the horse's physical development, it is imperative that you always strive to meet the following criteria:

- The horse moves forward freely with reaching, elastic strides.

- The horse is relaxed.

- The highest point of a horse's topline should be his poll, not the portion of his neck that is several inches behind the poll, as this indicates the horse has dropped behind the vertical.

- The horse's faceline is appropriate for his conformation and level of training: as much as 30 degrees in front of the vertical for inexperienced horses; 20 degrees for the beginning horse; 15 for the intermediate horse; 0 to 10 degrees for the advanced horse.

The training period can be scheduled in many different ways. It can take place as a continuous program either year-round or from spring through fall. Or the very beginning lessons can take place during a 30-day period. Then the horse can be turned out for a few months or an entire winter, and when returned to work, the training can resume. In total, it will take from several months to several years to accomplish the goals outlined in this book. Each horse will respond in his own time frame according to his starting point, his natural ability, and the ability of his trainer.

Obedience

The overall goal is to have your horse do what you want him to do, where you want him to do it, and when you want him to do it. Of course, your requests must be fair and reasonable at all times. If you make it easy for your horse to do the right thing, he will develop a positive attitude toward his work. If you set things up so that it is physically or mentally difficult for him to do the right thing, he may not look forward to his work. This does not mean that you shouldn't challenge your horse. By all means, he needs to be challenged in order to learn, but present him with requests that he can fill.

Often what a trainer asks of a young horse is the very opposite of what the horse would choose to do on his own. A young horse is frequently unfit, unbalanced, and emotionally unstable. This causes him to travel heavy on the forehand, crooked, and in a haphazard and erratic fashion. We aim to develop steadiness in a young horse. First we teach him what he should and should not do, and then we gradually improve his form in these maneuvers. When we define *how* a horse does what we want him to do, we are talking about the *quality* of his actions. To give the most solid base for more advanced work your young horse should work in harmony with you, moving freely forward with energy in a rhythmic, balanced fashion.

Freedom of Movement

When applied to horses, the word *free* can create confusion in some people's minds. Freedom indicates a lack of restriction and usually brings to mind a horse galloping through a field of flowers on a sunny day. Yet *free* is not necessarily synonymous with *wild*. A well-trained and disciplined horse can and should move freely. When used to describe a horse being trained, *free* refers to working him with effective aids that result in obedience without being forceful or physically inhibiting. The freely moving horse shows expression in his face, body carriage, and the way in which he lifts his legs, moves his shoulders, and uses his back. To be able to work a horse freely yet totally under control is the ultimate goal of riding, and can be achieved in varying degrees by all dedicated trainers.

To allow a horse freedom, the aids must be applied with correct timing, position, and intensity. It takes years for a trainer to refine the means to influence a horse without restricting or blocking the energy flowing around the horse's body.

Harmony

There must be harmony between a trainer and a horse in order for the energy to flow smoothly from horse to trainer. There must always be an open line of communication. To achieve harmony, on some days you may need to acknowledge your state of mind and admit that a change in your attitude might have to take place in order to have a productive training session. Harmony is evident in the expression and carriage of both the horse and trainer as they work. Poise, confidence, and pride in work are characteristics of horse and trainer harmony. If a trainer is tense, distracted, out of tune, or in a negative state of mind, the horse's performance will be negatively affected. A trainer and horse working in harmony are in a state of energized yet relaxed concentration and make the things they are doing together look smooth and effort-less.

Always observe your horse and determine whether he is responding to you or just reacting. Is he tuned in or tuned out?

Setting Goals

Goals are targets, the end results toward which you aim your actions. Goals increase incentive and fuel personal motivation. Horse competitions have fairly visible goals: the fastest time, the highest jump, the blue-ribbon ride. But behind each successful performance, there have been many at-home subgoals and objectives. Even if you are not competition-oriented, you should set goals. As a trainer, you will want to set immediate goals, short-term goals, and long-term (lifetime) goals for both you and your horse.

Immediate goals are usually very specific and measurable, such as, "I will longe my horse at a canter today without feeling as though I am water skiing!" or "Today I will introduce my horse to the surcingle."

Short-term goals can be thought of as those that are attainable within a specific time period. Depending on a horse's present level of training and your experience, your short-term goals might include, "I will be able to free-longe my horse at all gaits by the end of next month." Or "I will be ready to begin long lining in September."

Lifetime goals are understandably broader than immediate or short-term goals. They are often vague, even though they should not be: "I will become competent at all aspects of ground training," or "I will develop my longeing and long lining skills so that I will be able to instruct in those areas." Adding specifics makes a goal more measurable: "I will start at least four young horses every year to develop my ground-training skills," or "By the year XXXX, I will begin advertising my training services."

Did you notice that all statements are worded, "I will . . . " and not "I plan to . . . " or "I will try to . . . "? I feel that making positive statements is the best way to set goals with yourself and help yourself achieve them.

As you prepare to set your goals, be sure they are based on *you* becoming a better trainer than you presently are, rather than on you becoming better than another trainer is. Here, competition is not necessary and can be unhealthy. For you to win, it is not necessary that someone else loses. And just because someone else is successful does not mean that you have failed. Other people have different bodies, reflexes, horses, schedules, financial means, facilities, abilities, and, instructors than you have. If you compare your progress to someone else's, instead of focusing on your own progress, you can become frustrated, discouraged, unrealistic, and—as a result—you might place unfair demands on yourself and your horse. On the other hand, if you like to compare your progress to those obviously less experienced than yourself, you can develop a dangerous feeling of superiority, which can block your development and set you up for misfortunes and accidents.

Although the greatest amount of new-skill acquisition takes place when you first begin learning to longe or long line a horse, some people and some horses make only very minor, slow progress on a daily basis. And the more advanced you become as a trainer, the slower your progress may seem to be. You might be looking for that breakthrough you felt when you first began learning. So the best thing to do is compare your skill levels and understanding today to where you were yesterday. Keep a standard in mind and note the progress you make.

If other people (such as your parents or spouse) will be involved somehow in the process of your reaching your goals, be sure to explain to them what you are planning. If business associates or family members will be required to invest money or time in your endeavor or will be affected by your expenditures of money and time, it is crucial to have their consent and willing cooperation.

Write Down Your Goals

Write down your goals in finely focused and specifically described terms. Broad, vague goals are less likely to be reached, as it is difficult to determine when you have reached them. It is important to write down your goals rather than just think about them. People with explicit, written goals usually outperform those without them. In this book, you will find many lists and specific progressions that you can follow to formulate your own list of specific ground-training goals.

Often a person is hesitant to write down goals because of fear of failure or fear of success. Since goals are dynamic, they are meant to change. That is part of the growth process. If you write down a goal and don't reach it, you haven't necessarily failed. Rather, what often happens is that the goal either was not set properly in the first place or it has evolved.

If you write down goals and constantly meet them, other people tend to have high expectations of you. You might feel that success puts pressure on you to maintain your high level of achievement. Or it might make you feel you have to explain to others why you change your goals and plans midcourse. Such feelings and occurrences are natural and nothing to fear. They are part of the learning and developmental process of becoming a horse trainer.

It is crucial that you take time and care when setting your goals. Your success depends on it.

How to Set a Goal

To begin setting a goal, write down your overall goal.

> To safely and productively longe my horse in side reins.

To keep your goal as detailed as possible, you will need to define *safely* and *productively.*

Safely means that neither my horse nor I get hurt. *Productively means that my horse accepts the contact* from the side reins and gradually develops his forward movement and body carriage in response to the side reins.

To close in on your goal, you should list its subgoals:

> Longeing at all gaits in both directions calmly.
>
> Carrying a bridle while being longed.
>
> Accepting the girth restriction of a surcingle.
>
> Accepting the side reins loosely attached to the bit.
>
> As the side reins are gradually shortened over a period of weeks, accepting contact with the bit.
>
> Developing better balance and evenness as a result of the use of side reins.

To narrow the focus of your goal even further, you should choose one subgoal and list its components.

Carrying a bridle while being longed:

1. Learning how to be bridled and unbridled without any resistance or large head movements.

2. Carrying a bit quietly without a noseband.

3. Accepting the addition of a noseband.

4. Wearing a bridle during work without trying to rub it off.

Choose one component of the subgoal: Bridling and unbridling my horse without any resistance or large head movements

Define your objectives for it. Your objectives are your means for reaching the subgoal. Write them in the present tense in a positive tone. Your objectives will usually fall into four categories:

- Attitudes you need to develop.
- Habits you need to develop.
- Skills you need to develop.
- Outside influences you need to control.

Your attitudes include your desire to reach your goal, how you will feel when you reach your goal, and what it looks like in your mind's eye as you reach your goal. That's why you must really want to reach the goal. If, for example, you don't really believe that it's an important step to teach a horse to be bridled and unbridled with no resistance or movement, then you don't believe in your goal or progression

and you have weakened your chance for success.

Attitude. I feel a cooperative smoothness between my horse and me as I present the bridle to him; he softly opens his mouth, and I slip the headstall over his ears. I see my horse's feet being absolutely still and his head staying in a comfortable position so I can easily bridle him. By bridling successfully, I've set the tone for a positive training session.

Your habits include a mental rehearsal of how you will prepare for your goal, what you will do to reach your goal, what you will not do to reach your goal, and what you will do if things go wrong. This would include the way you unbuckle the throatlatch, hold the reins, present the bridle to your horse, the way you retain control of him while you are bridling, as well as a plan for regaining control of the situation if the horse resists.

Habit. Every time I bridle my horse, I take my time. I have the bridle ready before I approach my horse. I accustom my horse to the procedure by being consistent in the way I approach him and handle him. I'm never in a hurry when I bridle my horse. As I work, I pause regularly so that neither my horse nor I get in a hurry. If my horse throws up his head or tries to get away, I stop, regain my composure and control, and begin again.

Your skill development includes body awareness, exercises, and motor skills that you will practice both before you handle a horse and while you are working with him. If you are teaching a young horse how to be bridled, it helps if you hone your skills with an experienced, cooperative horse. That way you can focus on the exact progression and body awareness areas you will need to use later with the young horse.

Skill Development. To bridle my horse, I must stand near his head facing the same direction he is facing. I need to use the fingers of my left hand near his teeth and possibly need to put my thumb and middle finger in the interdental space to get him to open his mouth. Then, in one smooth move, I need to lift and position the bridle in his mouth and place the crownpiece behind his ears. I will practice bridling and unbridling a seasoned horse until my skills are smooth and rehearsed.

Then I will bridle and unbridle my young horse at least three or four times every day. I'll bridle him in his stall, unbridle him, and give him a pat. I won't always bridle him in association with a work session. Once he is confident in the procedure, I'll practice bridling him in different locations and from slightly different positions.

Outside influences include such things as proper equipment, footing, and factors in the external environment. It's best to hold bridling lessons in a secure area, free from distractions. If your horse happens to get away from you while you are bridling, you would be better off in a box stall than out in the stable yard. And to help your horse focus on what you are asking him to learn, it's best to find a quiet time and place for the first lessons. If you are in the aisle of a busy barn with vacuums going, dogs darting here and there, and doors opening and closing, there are too many other things for your horse to pay attention to.

Controlling Outside Influences. Before I begin, I'll check to see that the stall is safe and there is no commotion to distract us.

Plan the Work, then Work the Plan

Once you have zeroed in on your goals, start heading toward them. It is imperative that you believe in what you are doing. Begin now, not later this afternoon, tomorrow, or after New Year's. Procrastinate and you vegetate. If you need to bolster your incentive, itemize the benefits that reaching your goal will bring.

Positive Statements

Some people find positive statements useful for keeping on track. A positive statement about your objectives can be thought, spoken, or written on a regular basis as you work toward your goal. Positive statements are part of the private conversations you have with yourself. You need to devise, plant, and sustain positive statements to fit your personal beliefs and feelings. Some statements tend to be very specific and businesslike: "If I keep my horse between my driving arm that holds the whip and my restraining arm that holds the longe line, I can control my horse in any gait."

Others are imaginative and introspective: "As I long line my horse, I feel as if we are dancing partners in an elegant and unique ballet."

If you find that your mind has negative responses when you try to use positive statements, seize the opportunity to see exactly what stands between you and your goal. Often a negative reaction will vividly point out the obstacles standing in your way. For example, if using a positive statement makes you say, "This is for wimps!" it could indicate that you need a gentler approach to training. On the other hand, if reciting a statement makes you feel like a drill sergeant, perhaps you need more organization and discipline in your training. Your underlying tendencies will often be revealed in your reactions to positive statements.

As you work toward your longeing goals, allow yourself to be influenced only by healthy, positive, supportive people. Misery loves company, and often people unintentionally try to drag other people down to their level of frustration or dissatisfaction. Stay focused and positive, and plan to work mostly on your own. If you are lucky enough to have a friend who is also positive and directed, be supportive of him or her.

Anticipate problems that may occur along the way to your goal. Work out the solutions ahead of time and carry them around in your head so you can institute them quickly. You will need to know how to make sound decisions when problems surface, and with ground training there are plenty of surprises.

When you make a decision, you determine what type of action is to be taken and when. To make an effective decision you must be informed, observant, expedient but not hasty, and ready to take action. The action can be designed to correct a problem, prevent a problem, or temporarily bring a problem to a closure until the proper action can be determined. Or an action can replace Plan A, a previous decision and action, with Plan B, a more-likely-to-succeed solution. Rather than be carried along aimlessly, stay focused, and make decisive steps as you work toward your objectives.

It helps if you keep records so that you can evaluate where you have been, where you are, and where you are headed. Photographs, videotapes, and journals can all provide specific benchmarks for you to use periodically in evaluating your horse's progress. Be observant and flexible so that as you evaluate you can make necessary changes and restructure your program.

If in your review, you find that your original plan is no longer appropriate, revise it and move on to a new plan. Be sure that you take time out for mental and physical recharging when it is necessary, so that you come back with renewed energy and enthusiasm.

The Time Crunch

Horse owners universally state that the most limiting factor in achieving their goals is the lack of time. It is a fact that training and caring for horses requires a good deal of time. Often, though, when a person says she lacks time, what she really lacks is quality time. Quality time is characterized by focused, productive work. It is not how much you get done that is important but how well you do what you do.

To ensure that the time spent with your horse is quality time, don't be in a hurry as you work with him. Your goal-setting exercises will help you determine what to do. Do first things first. It's better to do simple things well than to bumble through more advanced lessons. Focus on what you are doing so you do things right the first time and don't create large, time-consuming problems. Finish what you start.

Be orderly; it will save you immeasurable time. Have a place for everything and keep everything in its place. Use written and mental checklists to give you a measurable sense of completion.

Problems Trainers Commonly Face

Stress. Stress is a demand for adaptation. A certain amount of mental and physical stress is necessary for the development of a trainer and a horse. But when the amount or frequency of stress exceeds a healthy level, your reasoning, problem-solving ability, and effectiveness decline. An overdose of stress may cause irreversible damage to your physical and emotional reserves. Get in touch with your stress barometer so you know how much is just enough and how much is too much. Know when to take a break or get help.

Tension and fear. Horses are very sensitive and can easily detect a fearful or tense trainer. Every horse's reaction to tension and fear is slightly different, but reactions may include biting, kicking, running, shying, rearing, stiffening, and balking. Fear in a trainer is usually a result of a previous wreck in which trainer and/or horse got hurt; it might be fear of failure, fear of looking or being incompetent, fear of "ruining" the horse. The closer you follow safety guidelines and are consistent in your handling methods, the less you have to fear. Ask yourself these questions related to your fears: Are you physically or mentally unable to perform what you are attempting? Do you have an instructor who can give you feedback on your training? Are you practicing regularly? Have you been badly hurt? Have you felt embarrassed in front of others? Are you keeping your progress with your horse training in proper perspective with the rest of your life?

Plateaus. What kind of picture comes to mind when you hear the word "plateau"? A plateau can be a resting spot where you rejuvenate and regroup, or a level, clear, elevated place to hone your skills by practicing what you already know. To some it indicates a stale place where one gets stuck.

There is nothing wrong with being on a plateau—it might be the perfect time to schedule an official rest period for the benefit of both you and your horse. Similarly, if you see that your schedule will cause your upcoming training sessions to be irregular and of poor quality, plan an official period of R and R. Hang up the long lines and turn your horse out for a week or so. When it's time to resume, you will most likely find that both you and your horse approach the work with more gusto and interest. Right now, I am on a plateau, writing this book. The winter winds are whistling and my horses are snug in their turn-out blankets. We are all looking forward to resuming a regular training program in just a few weeks.

With longeing, especially, it is possible to get stuck on a plateau and practice a certain level of longeing for a long time. It might be work that comes easy but is not necessarily very productive. If you find yourself getting casual or bored, you can bet your horse is, too. Repeating things that you know well is a natural tendency, and it serves at least one important purpose. Doing those things that come easily and can be performed well allows you to develop skills and a feeling for the aids.

If you find you have slipped into a rut, however, it might be symbolic of the mental stagnation you and your horse are feeling. Repeating the same maneuver over and over again, especially if the horse is

doing it well, can bore the horse, dull his responsiveness and willingness, and keep you from progressing.

If you find yourself repeating the same things over and over again because you do not know how to solve an upcoming problem or don't know what to work on next, then a plateau can represent a frustrating standstill. But frustration can also be a powerful motivator for learning and improvement.

As you progress in your training and confidence, you will find yourself spending less time on the familiar, comfortable things and more time on things that challenge both you and your horse. You might focus on advanced long line maneuvers or a more specialized use for your groundwork, such as preparing for a trail class.

If you find that even successful training sessions have a staleness to them, then you might just be experiencing general fatigue due to overwork in all areas of your life. If you lose interest or enthusiasm in the work, have slow reflexes, or are tired or irritable, examine the rest of your life— the part that has nothing to do with horses—first. Although poor diet, inadequate sleep, home worries, or excessive school or workload may cause staleness, it can also be the result of excess emotional tension caused by intense involvement in some other aspect of your life. The best way to come out of a stale period is to participate in a diversionary playful activity—perhaps an activity that you have never pur-sued before and that has nothing to do with horses. It could be traveling. When you return to your training, bring with you that sense of play. If staleness presents itself regularly, it may be a sign that you need to reexamine the reason you have a horse or lighten the intensity of the goals you have set for yourself.

Goals as You Longe Your Horse

General Goals

Expression and attitude are just as important as mechanics. As you work your horse on the longe line, aim to develop his gaits so they are pure and unhurried but with plenty of energy from the hindquarters. If you allow a horse to rush or work with an uneven or impure rhythm, that rhythm will carry over to his saddle work. Influencing the tempo of a horse's gaits on the longe line is one of the most difficult aspects of longeing. You must encourage energy and action from the horse, using your body language and the whip, while at the same time containing it with the action of your body and the longe line.

Obedience and the impulsion and purity of the gaits are the most important aspects of early longeing. Only after the horse has learned to be cooperative and move forward with energy and a consistent rhythm would you attempt to introduce the bridle and side reins.

TRAINING GOALS IN THEIR APPROXIMATE ORDER OF CONCERN

1. *Forward impulsion.* The desire to actively move forward. The thrust or manner in which the horse's weight is settled and released from the supporting structures of the limb in the act of carrying the horse forward. The aids that drive the horse forward and encourage forward impulsion include body language, voice commands, and whip position. Forward impulsion is discouraged by the improper or early use of any type of headgear. Forward

impulsion is the single most effective problem preventative and problem solver in all aspects of longeing, long lining, and riding. Moving a horse forward often straightens out the problem immediately.

2. *Relaxation.* Relaxation is the absence of excess muscular tension. Suppleness and flexibility are dependent on the horse being relaxed. Excess muscular tension leads to fear, quickness, and injury.

3. *Rhythm.* The steadier a horse's rhythm, the more relaxed and balanced he is. Steady rhythm is composed of several elements. *Rhythm*, per se, is the cadence of the footfall within a gait, taking into account timing (number of beats) and accent of the beats. *Evenness* is the balance, symmetry, and synchronization of the steps within a gait in terms of weight bearing and timing. *Regularity* is the cadence, the rhythmical precision with which each stride is taken in turn. *Tempo* is the rate of movement, the rate of stride repetition; a faster tempo results in more strides per minute.

4. *Overall Balance.* The harmonious, precise, coordinated form of a horse's movement is referred to as *balance*. It is composed of equal distribution of weight from the left side of the horse's body to the right and an appropriate relationship between the weight-bearing functions of the forehand and the hindquarters.

5. *Lateral Balance and Bending.* Circles and circular figures require turning. The turn can involve an almost imperceptible arcing of the horse's spine on a very large circle or an extreme inward curving for a sharp, collected movement such as a quarter turn. Turning requires proper flexion and bending.

Lateral flexion is a turn of the horse's head to one side or the other. The movement takes place at the joint of the axis vertebrae; the junction of the neck and the head, more commonly referred to as the poll or throatlatch area. When a horse is described as flexed (in contrast to bent), the rest of his spine (from the poll to the tail) is straight. Flexion is created with side rein aids in longeing and with long lines in ground driving. There can be lateral flexion without lateral bend, as in the case of leg yielding. Generally, however, a horse who is flexed is also bent.

Lateral bend is the arcing of the horse's entire body. When circling right, the horse will be bent to the right. Correct lateral bend requires lateral flexion. The bend must be uniform from poll to tail. The horse's neck is more flexible than the back, so the tendency is for the front of the horse to overbend. This can be one of the main problems with side rein use and must be avoided.

6. *Solid, Forward Transitions.* A transition is a shifting of gears. Most commonly, an *upward* transition indicates a change from a standstill or a slower gait to a gait that is more ground-covering. Examples are halt to walk, walk to trot, trot to canter, and walk to canter. In addition, an upward transition can indicate a change in the movement within a gait. For example, a trot can be regular (often called *working*), extended, or collected. The change from a working trot or a collected trot to an extended trot would be considered an upward transition.

A *downward* transition is a change from a gait that is more ground covering or faster to one that is less so. Examples are canter to trot, canter to walk, trot to walk, and walk to

halt. Downward transitions can also indicate decreases within a gait, such as a decrease from extended canter to collected canter.

Good transitions are prompt yet not sudden. A horse *must* be prepared for every transition. No transition is correct without the proper use of preparatory commands.

Transitions are a smooth balance between driving aids and restraining aids. Although the net result of these forces should be near zero, indicating that they approach being equal, there should always be a tendency for more driving energy so the transitions are forward.

7. *Variation within the gaits.* The variations within gaits—such as working trot, extended trot, collected trot—should be distinct transitions. The goal is that the tempo remain the same for the variations within a gait.

8. *Straightness.* Only through straightening can a horse learn to move in the balance necessary for every horse performance. When worked in a circular figure, he must travel "straight" on that figure. His entire body must be bent according to the line he is working on, but his hind legs must follow in the

---

STRAIGHT OR CROOKED?

The majority of horses move naturally "crooked," as it requires less effort than moving straight. Most training strives for *ordinary straightness,* in which the spine (midline) is in a straight line. Because a horse's hips are wider than his shoulders, the hind feet do not step directly in the tracks of the front when the horse is straight by ordinary standards. Dressage strives for *relative straightness,* in which the inside hind follows in the exact track of the inside front.

Most horses (80 to 90 percent) travel naturally crooked in this fashion: The right hind travels in a track to the right of the right front, and so sends more weight diagonally to the left shoulder, causing the horse to fall in to the left. The left hind leg carries more weight, and the right hind pushes the body to the left. This results in the left side being stiffer and stronger than the right side. So, when going to the left, the horse overbends to the left, weights the left shoulder, and swings the hindquarters off the track to the right.

When going to the right, the horse almost always counterflexes to the left (counterbends with a straight stiffness), which results in strong contact on the right rein and the hindquarters swinging in to the right.

About 10 to 20 percent of horses travel crooked in the opposite way.

---

tracks of his front legs. When a horse is worked in a circle, his inside hind leg carries more weight than the outside one.

9. *Vertical Flexion.* Vertical flexion is a characteristic of collection, one aspect of advanced training. It refers to the upward arching of the horse's spine (as evidenced by a rounded back, dropped croup, curved neck, elevated poll, face line approaching the vertical), and the increased flexion of the limb joints (most noticeably the knees and hocks).

The Gaits

A gait is any of the footfall patterns of a horse, such as a walk, trot, canter, or gallop. A gait is like a simple musical piece written in its own specific time. Every horse expresses each gait in his own particular

WHICH SIDE FIRST? STRONGER OR WEAKER?

Should a horse be longed first and/or longer on his strong side or weak side?

Horses, like humans, usually have a side preference. That is why most horses initially travel stiff in one direction and overbent in the other. This is often referred to as a horse's natural stiffness and hollowness or a horse's strong and weak sides. Many horses are stiffer (stronger) on the left side of their bodies. That is, the left sides of their bodies tend to curl inward to the left and strongly resist stretching to the right or straightening. When such a horse travels to the left, its strong left side may tend to overcurl the horse to the inside, with head lower and tipped down. The majority of the horse's weight is borne on the left shoulder. It will be difficult for the horse to keep even contact on the reins. When traveling to the right, the same horse will have difficulty counteracting the strong left pull from the left side of the body, so will have difficulty bending to the right. This can show up in several ways: Usually the head is up, carried to the left, the body held at an angle with the front feet outside the tracks

of the hind feet, the hindquarters shifted in to the right, weight falling out on the left shoulder. If made to bend to the right, such a horse would probably overbend to the right and bulge (or pop) out its left shoulder, or carry its entire body to the left to relieve the stress from the stretch on the left side. Until a horse is systematically developed, he often has a difficult time bending his entire body uniformly in both directions.

So, at the beginning, it's best to start longeing on the horse's stronger side, which is usually the left. That way, during the warm-up, fewer new problems are likely to pop up. After warm-up, you can switch to the weaker side but you may find, at first, that you can't work the horse as long in this direction. As the lessons progress, you will gradually increase the amount of time the horse can work to the weaker side, and eventually you will be able to start some of the sessions on the weaker side. Remember that developmental exercises are not by nature confrontational. They are gradual progressions to a desired state, not a showdown.

tempo and style. Some horses have one or two gaits that do not have an even, precise rhythm. The goal of ground-training exercises is to develop a regular rhythm in each gait and thereby develop the purity of the gait. Longeing and long lining provide you with a great opportunity for observing gaits.

A *working gait* is the ordinary gait of an average horse who is moving in balance and with a regular rhythm and average impulsion.

A *collected gait* is performed at the same tempo as the working gait but has a shorter, more elevated stride with a longer support phase, and therefore covers less ground than a working gait. Collection is brought about by a shift of the center of gravity rearward and is usually accompanied by an overall body elevation and an increase in joint flexion.

An *extended gait* is performed at the same tempo as the working gait but has a longer stride with more reach and an increased period of suspension, and therefore covers more ground than a working gait. Extension is brought about by a driving force from behind and a reaching in front; usually accompanied by a horizontal floating called "suspension." *Suspension* is the horizontal floating that occurs when a limb is extended and the body continues moving forward; the word also refers to the moment at the canter and gallop when all limbs are flexed or curled up, reorganizing for the next stride. A

lengthening is a stage on the way to an extended gait.

Walk

The walk is a four-beat gait that should have a clear, even rhythm as the feet land and take off in the following sequence: left hind, left front, right hind, right front. The walk has alternating lateral and triangular bases of support. At one moment, the horse's weight is borne by two left legs, and then the right hind is added, forming a triangle of support. Later in the cycle, all weight is borne by the two right legs. That's why the walk creates a side-to-side and front-to-back motion. A Western horse who really walks out with good forward energy is said to have a "rein-swinging" walk. A dressage horse should walk with head and neck unconstrained and lightly on the bit. The speed of the average walk is about four miles per hour. The footprints of the hinds should at least touch or land partially on top of the front prints, but it's better if they are in front of the imprints of the forefeet.

An extended walk is a lengthening but not a quickening of the walk stride. The horse's hindquarters, head and neck, and forelegs all reach forward. Contact with the bit is maintained. If you examine the hoof prints, each hind foot should reach beyond the print of its corresponding forefoot.

A collected walk has shorter steps and covers less ground but has the same four-beat rhythm as the working walk. The collected walk has a crisp cadence, more like marching. Because of the shorter stride, there is no overstepping of the hind prints on the front tracks. The hinds touch slightly behind the imprints of the front feet. The limb joints are more acute and springy.

A free walk is characterized by long strides, a relaxed back, and a lowered head and neck. This is usually on a long or loose line with no contact or very light contact. In either case, the horse should be allowed to carry his head and neck as low as he likes. The free walk is a good way to check whether the previous work has been correct.

Trot

The trot is a two-beat diagonal gait where the right front and left hind legs (called the "right diagonal") rise and fall together, and the left front and right hind legs (called the "left diagonal") rise and fall together. Between the landings of the diagonal pairs there is a moment of suspension, which results in a springy gait. The working trot is an active, ground-covering trot. The average speed of a working trot is six to eight miles per hour. The hind feet should step into the tracks of the front feet.

"Trot" refers to the gait as performed under English tack, with a greater length of stride and impulsion than the Western jog, which is shorter strided and has minimal suspension. The jog is usually performed on a loose rein with a great deal of relaxation.

Since the jog and sitting trot are usually the steadiest and most stable and rhythmic of a horse's gaits, they are useful for developing the horse's rhythm and are the cornerstones of many exercises for the horse's training.

The extended trot is at the same tempo as the working trot, except that the horse has longer strides, really reaching with the front legs, pushing and driving with the hindquarters with great impulsion. This trot has the longest moment of suspension, and therefore covers the most ground possible as the horse glides through the air. There should be a great overstep of the hind feet over the prints of the front feet. There is a distinct lengthening of the frame with the nose stretching forward and down somewhat.

The collected trot is performed at the same tempo as the working trot but with shorter steps, more marked cadence, more joint flexion, a rounded back, well-engaged hindquarters, and—subsequently—a naturally (not forced) elevated neck and more vertical flexion in the poll. This is an energetic trot with the balance shifted rearward, which allows free shoulder movement. This trot has the shortest moment of suspension; therefore, it covers the least ground and the hind feet usually do not reach the imprints of the front feet.

Canter

The canter (lope) is a three-beat gait with the following footfall pattern:

1. Initiating hind leg or outside hind.

2. The diagonal pair or inside hind and outside foreleg.

3. Leading foreleg or inside foreleg.

4. Regrouping of legs or a moment of suspension.

When the initiating hind leg is the left, the diagonal pair will consist of the right hind and the left front; the leading foreleg will be the right front, and the horse will be on the right lead. When you observe a horse on the right lead from the side, his right legs will reach farther forward than his left legs. The right hind will reach under his belly farther than the left hind; the right front will reach out in front of his body farther than the left front. When he turns to the right, normally the horse should be on the right lead.

The canter has alternating rolling and floating aspects. The energy rolls from rear to front; then, during a moment of suspension, the horse gathers his legs up underneath himself to get organized for the next set of leg movements. The horse seems to glide for a moment until the initiating hind lands and begins the cycle again.

A lope is a relaxed version of the canter with less rein contact and a lower overall body carriage.

The extended canter displays a long, strong stride with head and neck reaching forward. This canter is horizontal, in contrast to the vertical nature of the collected canter. The extended canter has maximum ground coverage per stride while retaining the tempo of the working canter.

In the collected canter the strides are shorter, the legs move higher, and there is more joint folding (flexion) than in the working canter. The head and neck are up and flexed and the hindquarters are well under the horse's body. The horse's position creates the impression that he is cantering uphill.

Preparation for a Successful Session

Always turn a horse out for free exercise before longeing. This might seem like an odd notion because "longeing is exercise." But to the horse, you want the association to be "longeing is training." Therefore, if you want a horse to be able to pay attention, first he must burn off his excess energy with turn-out. Longeing is a time for learning, not playing. You do not want a horse to buck, run, or pull when you are handling him, so let him blow off steam before the lesson. The horse's turn-out should take place in an area other than the longeing pen. This will help to make a strong association between training areas and certain rules. In a training area, there should be no rolling, bucking, or kicking. In a turn-out area, anything goes. The ideal turn-out area is a one-acre grassy paddock with good footing.

If you find your horse is just too full of energy to really pay attention and work, perhaps you are feeding him a ration that is too high in energy. Decrease the amount of grain. Otherwise you might find that you have to work your horse so long and hard to burn off his energy that he will be physically fatigued by the time he is mentally ready to pay attention. Working a horse after he is really fatigued can lead to injury and a sour attitude.

If, on the other hand, your horse is dull and not attentive and plays out after just a short work, he may not be getting adequate energy from his feed. There are many other health-related factors that can cause low-energy behavior. Refer to the "Recommended Reading" section at the end of the book for more information on these topics.

How long should you longe your horse? It will vary from 5 minutes for the first lessons for a young horse to 45 minutes for a well-trained, well-conditioned horse who is perhaps receiving a longe session instead of riding. Remember that the continuous circling of longeing can be stressful, so you don't want to longe a horse too frequently or for too long a time.

Much more can be accomplished in a short but well-planned lesson than during a haphazard, long, tiring, problematic session. It is not how long you work but the quality of the work that is important.

Guidelines for a Training Session

General Thoughts

The goal of horse training is to bend the horse rather than break him. Presenting the horse with progressive, well-planned lessons will alter his behavior in subtle ways. That is the art of horse training.

A horse is much more secure when his role is made perfectly clear. When you're planning a training session, it is best to have a very specific order of events in mind. Although you need to be flexible within the preestablished plan, each training session should have a realistic goal.

Distractions prevent a horse from giving his full attention to the lesson. For example, it is best to eliminate dogs from the training area, postpone lawn mowing, and reschedule the turn-out of rambunctious weanlings in the adjacent pasture if you plan to work with a horse who is very young or inexperienced. Eventually, the horse should perform regardless of distractions, but initially, a horse learns faster when he can concentrate on the trainer and the lesson.

One trainer for one horse reduces confusion over aids. We all do things slightly differently. Once the horse has become steady in his responses, however, it is wise to begin exposing him to other competent handlers so that he develops a tolerance for slight variations in routine.

It is counterproductive to rush during a training session. You need to take the time to move through the progressive steps of a maneuver. Teaching the horse one thing at a time is only logical and fair. Your movements around horses should be smooth, but not necessarily slow.

Expect the best from each training session, but be prepared to deal with the worst. With a positive attitude, approach the training arena with the appropriate equipment and safety principles in mind. Playing out the "worst-case scenario" in your mind ahead of time will help you visualize what to do if things do go wrong.

If things are not working, change something. Be tactful yet effective. Many options are outlined in this book and in *101 Longeing and Long Lining Exercises.*

Portions of a Training Session

A typical training session includes preparation of the horse (which may require turn-out), warm-up of horse, the new work, cool-down, and post-work care of the horse.

Using one hour as an example, if you schedule 10 minutes for a warm-up and plan to save 10 minutes for a cool-down, you have 40 minutes left for the new work. You could apportion the 40 minutes this way: review work 10 minutes; break 2 minutes; new work 15 minutes; break 3 minutes; review work 10 minutes. Then it would be time for the cool-down.

Preparation of the Horse

The training of your horse begins with the first step you take toward him to catch him. As you lead your horse to the grooming area, stay in proper position in the vicinity of the horse's shoulder and be direct and precise in your body language.

Tie the horse or attach him to crossties so he is safe for you to work on while you are grooming and tacking him. If it is fly season, you may need to begin by lightly spraying the legs with a fly repellent. This will make it safer for you to work around his legs.

Put on a pair of barn gloves and begin by picking out the hooves. Continue grooming the horse by loosening dirt, hair, and dead skin and scurf from his skin with a rubber curry on all the muscled portions of the horse. Use a soft rubber grooming tool or mitt to perform a similar function on the horse's head and legs. Then with a stiff-bristled brush, whisk the loosened debris from the body with a flicking motion of your wrist. (At this stage of grooming, long, sweeping brush strokes would only serve to relocate the dirt.) Use a brush of medium to soft stiffness on the head and legs. Once most of the dirt is removed, use a soft brush to finish the coat with long, smooth strokes. Set the coat and remove any dust with a dry or damp cloth.

Tack up the horse according to his level of training.

When you reach the arena, stop the horse straight and square, and give him the command to stand. Routinely take your time preparing to start the lesson, as this practice will develop patience in your horse. You will need to organize your longe line, attach side reins if you are

TYPES OF WORK

FORWARD WORK Energetic walk and long trot on large circles with minimal contact and minimal bending. This is the work for a warm-up and cool-down, and in the early stages of training can be the sole work for both the review sessions and new work.

GYMNASTICS Forward work with bending, such as large circles, large change of rein turns, serpentines. This work is appropriate for the last part of the warm-up, the review periods, and the new work.

CONNECTED WORK Precollection work involving longitudinal flexion, such as walk-trot, trot-walk, trot-canter, and canter-trot transitions (all using side reins), and backing in long lines. Generally this work should be covered during the new work period.

using them, and check to see that bridle and surcingle are straight and properly adjusted. Give the cinch, or girth, its final tightening. Put on your gloves, sunglasses, and secure your hat. Stand for just a moment without doing a thing. When you decide it is time to move off, give your horse the appropriate signals.

The Warm-Up

A warm-up decreases the chance of tissue damage from sudden, unusual stresses. It readies the neurological pathways, alerting them for signals, thereby increasing coordination during the more demanding work that will follow. A warm-up increases the blood flow to the skeletal muscles, which increases their strength of contraction and allows muscles to stretch without damage. Stretching exercises should not be used as the first part of a warm-up, however, as they may result in torn fibers.

At first, use a watch to keep track of the time as you work. You will learn to read a horse's signs and know when it is time to move on to the next segment of the session. Every horse has a different peak period capacity, which will increase as his condition improves. The peak is the point at which his mind, nerves, and muscles are honed and ready to perform at their best. Know how long your horse's peak will last and work to that point only. If you insist that he work past his peak, you risk destroying what you have gained in the previous work. And don't use up all your horse's energy in the warm-up—be sure to save some gas for the new work.

From this point forward, a six-year-old gelding with average longeing skills is used to depict the portions of a training session. He is accustomed to the bridle, cavesson, surcingle, and side reins. He is a mellow and sometimes lazy horse who has to "warm up" mentally to the idea of work.

The principles outlined here are the same for a horse at any level of training. Comments on the horse's form are explained in more detail in chapters 6 and 7.

It is beneficial to move the horse at a walk on loose-line and side-rein contact for at least 2 to 3 minutes before starting to work at a trot. This prevents the bad habits of anticipation and allows the horse to warm up gradually.

The Work

When you are ready to begin the work session, begin with a review of something your horse knows well and is capable of performing with relative ease. It might be simply a quiet trot. It should be active, forward work with the horse working in a large circle.

When it's time to first trot the horse, keep the side-rein contact loose so the horse has a chance to prepare mentally and physically for the idea of moving forward. At first the horse might move lazily, with very little reach of the hind legs and a hollow topline, as in the photo (Photo 2.1).

2.1 *The beginning of a typical session: the horse is wearing a longeing cavesson, bridle, surcingle, and loose side reins. He starts out with short strides at the trot, hollow back, and head high. Lazy and unfocused.*

Adjust the side reins to a length that is appropriate for the horse's level of experience (Photo 2.2). With a young horse, such an adjustment is very gradual. With a more experienced horse, you might find you can "go" to his optimum setting right after the warm-up.

With the reins shortened just a hole or two, this gelding "wakes up" and starts

2.2 *After having a chance to warm up, he is brought to a halt and the side reins are adjusted for working contact.*

2.4 *After a few rounds, he finds a way to move forward with energy (note improved trot stride length), light contact on the bit (side reins are still a bit slack), yet his nose is in front of the vertical (good sign) and his poll is the highest point of his topline (good). He is not overbending to the left, as in an imbalance common with most horses.*

2.3 *He returns to work with a renewed sense of energy, depicted by the longer stride at the trot. He is looking for balance, however, as evidenced by the low poll and slack side reins.*

to go to work, which is evidenced by a greater forward drive with his hindquarters (Photo 2.3). But carrying his weight

on his hindquarters requires more work, and he has not yet fully warmed up to the idea of "balance." He has let his weight fall on his forehand, as evidenced by his poll being the lowest point of his topline.

After just a few minutes, he shows even more drive from the hindquarters. His elevated neck and poll are evidence that more of his weight has shifted from his forehand to his hindquarters (Photo 2.4). His nose is slightly in front of the vertical, he is slightly counterflexed (out of the circle), and his topline is a bit hollow; but all in all this is a more energized and correctly balanced form than that in the preceding photo.

After some good work at the trot, the gelding is brought down to a walk to assess his level of energy (Photo 2.5). He continues to step well under himself with his hind legs, his topline is ideal, and his face line is a few degrees in front of the vertical, which is desirable at the walk. If he had dropped his head, suddenly to the ground or raised it high or wagged it side-to-side or shut down his impulsion by taking tiny mincing steps, it would have shown that the work was incorrect and incomplete and he wasn't ready to work in the next direction.

You will know that your horse has had proper work when he blows (exhales through his nose), breathes long and deep, when he mouths the bit, and begins lowering his head yet reaches forward with his neck, as in the photo. Almost any horse improves after a warm-up. The lazy horse's blood gets flowing and he becomes more physically stimulated to work. The hyperactive, hot horse gets the edges smoothed off frenetic neuromuscular signals, which results in smoother, more controlled movements.

2.5 *Even at the walk, he maintains good form. The side reins are not so short as to be inappropriate for the walk. Ideally his poll should be an inch higher, but it's lowered because this is a very relaxed walk and his weight has fallen on his forehand a little.*

When you take a rest break, take care not to let the horse just dump his weight on his forehand. Let him, instead, gradually stretch down. If a horse stretches down, it indicates that the review work was successful. Let him mosey forward and blow a little. As the rest period comes to a close, adjust the side reins if necessary and drive him forward again until you have him working in the state he was in before the break.

Introducing New Work

The new work period should include more difficult work, such as a series of transitions, spirals, turns, or collected work. The new work period is concentrated and should not be too long. How long? That is an art and a science. Although you'd like to make a breakthrough during every session, that isn't a realistic expectation. Sometimes you need to quit while you are ahead. If a horse has given an honest effort but begins to tire and make mistakes, it is time to move out of the new work period and into the final review, or even directly to the cool-down. On the other hand, if a horse is being belligerent, and refuses to listen, then you may need to work him through the difficulty. Rather than fight, walk him on a long rein for a moment, rearrange your thoughts, and then return to the work. Once your horse is in good physical condition and you know his level of mental concentration, you may recognize at certain times that things are going so well you can ask for more complex things. When introducing new things, however, there always is the potential for running into a problem. You will have to decide whether you need to resolve a problem or bring the session to a tactful closure and deal with the problem during the next session.

When it is time to change direction, if you are using a bridle with or without side reins, you will have to stop the horse, change the setting on the reins and the attachment of the longe line, and turn him in-hand. Now, don't think that just because the work was quite nice in the first direction, when you turn the horse the other way, there will be an automatic carryover of benefits. It does not always work that way. In fact, when sent to the right, the horse might be more hollow, lazy, and counterflexed than he was to the left!

But with side-rein adjustment and active driving aids from body language, voice commands, and whip position, the horse begins moving actively forward, even though his poll has dropped again (Photo 2.6). Notice that almost always, when the poll drops, the hind legs are not driving deeply. That characteristic is typical of a horse who is traveling heavily on his forehand. With additional time to warm up and some added driving aids, the horse comes up in front and drives more deeply from behind.

During canter work, and especially on the depart, a horse will curl up too much

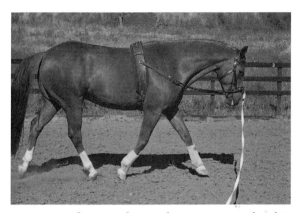

2.6 *When we change direction, note that he has counterflexed a little bit to the left. His poll is low and he is not stepping under himself as well as to the left.*

2.7 *One way to elevate the forehand and get the hind to drive and the back to round is with canter work. Notice that the goals have been accomplished.*

to the inside, even though this makes him take more contact with the outside rein than the inside one, which often is slack. Once a horse adds more impulsion to his canter work, he lengthens his topline and his stride comes up in front, and carries himself straight on the circle (Photo 2.7). Here it appears that there is almost a tendency to counterflex to the outside of the circle, but this is partly due to the perspective and partly due to the fact that the horse is cantering on a circle of more than 20 meters (65 feet) in diameter, so his body looks "straight," as it should on a circle that large.

The break after the new work is a little bit longer than the previous break, but it is similar in format. Remember that a horse's desire to stretch is a result of well-done connected work. Once you have picked your horse back up, you will begin the final work session.

During the closing review period, it is best to identify the areas in which the horse may have had problems with the new work and go back to the basics that underlie them. Don't work on the new concept itself, but review and reestablish the pertinent foundation principles so that during the next training session the horse will have a better chance of performing the new work correctly. To preserve a horse's interest in his work, end with something he does well. It is also good for you to end with a good opinion of yourself and your training.

The Cool-Down

After a vigorous work session, it is important to let your horse gradually and systematically wind down from the work. Budget 10 to 15 minutes to accomplish this. The cool-down begins when you have given the horse some slack in the line and/ or side reins, and decreased your driving aids, and it ends when you have returned to the barn to untack.

The reins are loosened for the cool-down but the horse is not allowed to "die" (Photo 2.8). The driving aids are still requesting forward movement, which helps the muscles dispel the lactic acid from the more demanding work. When a work session is ending and the reins are long and loose and the horse carries himself in this form, it indicates that the work has been correct. If the horse had raised his head and hollowed his back and moved with short, choppy strides, it would indicate the work was incorrect and the horse is

2.8 *For the final walk during the cool-down period, the side reins are loosened so the horse can lower his head and reach forward. He is still walking fairly energetically.*

2.9 *It is a good sign when the horse stretches down to the ground as he continues to walk forward. This means the work has been correct.*

ending on a tense note rather than a relaxed one.

When the driving aids cease, the gelding knows he is invited and allowed to have a good downward stretch, which gives his topline a good, relaxing stretch (Photo 2.9). The fact that a horse will stretch low also indicates that there is a lack of tension at the end of the session.

The cool-down does not have to consist entirely of walking around on a long line. It can, and should for very fit horses, include some time trotting freely on a long line. That sort of loose, relaxed trotting will help flush from the dense muscles of the hindquarters the lactic acid that is especially prevalent after collected work. After particularly vigorous work, you may choose to loosen the surcingle and noseband or cavesson somewhat and lead your horse for the last 5 minutes either around the arena or in a paddock.

If your horse is very hot, do not let him cool out too quickly. Keep his back and loin covered with a quarter sheet or wool cooler while his muscles dissipate their heat via evaporation. Spraying a hot horse with cold water will cause his muscles to get stiff. Using water to hose sweat and dirt off your horse every day is not a good long-term management practice anyway. It can result in more problems than benefits. A daily wet/dry situation can be extremely damaging to the structure of your horse's hooves. Horses' hooves are heal-

thiest when they are exercised regularly but kept at a relatively constant dry external moisture level. Also, fungus and skin problems can occur when horses are frequently wetted down and aren't allowed to dry thoroughly.

One solution to cleaning a sweaty horse without hosing him down is to use a body wipe in specific areas such as the head, saddle area, the underside of the neck, and between the hind legs. Commercial body braces are available, or you can make your own by filling a gallon plastic milk container with water, adding two tablespoons of Calgon water softener, 2 tablespoons of baby oil, and one ounce of your favorite liniment. This mixture lifts dirt and sweat off the horse's hair, conditions it, and stimulates the skin. If your horse is very sensitive, you may need to decrease or eliminate the liniment from the formula. With any horse, do not use liniment near the eyes, nostrils, or on the anus.

After wiping your horse down, leave him tied so he can dry while you attend to your tack. Wipe the mouthpiece and rings of the bit with a damp cloth. Clean the leather portions of your tack with a liquid saddle soap—a spray bottle makes things easier. Use paste, bar, or gel saddle soap for weekly cleaning. Be careful not to spray the bit with the soapy solution. Wipe all the sweat and dirt from your tack each time you use it to prolong its life and prevent breakage.

After a sweaty workout, there is nothing a horse likes better than to roll in some soft dirt. Of course a dirty coat will create problems for you next time you want to ride, so the best bet is to put a sheet on the horse so that when he rolls he doesn't grind dirt into his coat. Letting him roll without a sheet in a grassy area, in a sandy pen, or in an area with sawdust or shavings is a good compromise. After he has had a chance to satisfy his act of self-grooming, brush him or vacuum him, cover him with a sheet, and return him to his stall or pen.

Protecting Yourself from the Elements

The better you take care of yourself, the longer you will last as a horse trainer. It's that simple!

Protect your feet by wearing well-made, sturdy boots (Photo 2.10). The boots should have heels, good traction, and if possible, an extra piece of leather sewn across the toe. This toe cap provides

2.10 *Safe, sturdy comfortable boots are essential for groundwork. You need good traction, toe protection, and something you can trot in if necessary.*

added protection if a horse should step on your foot.

Wear gloves when you handle ropes or lines. Leather gloves give you a better grip on ropes and protect your skin from the pain of a rope burn if the rope zings through your hand unexpectedly.

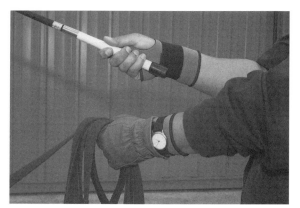

2.11 *Protect your hands with gloves, your wrists with supports. Wear a watch to time the sessions.*

I like to wear smooth leather gloves (shown here on the left hand; just for the photo I did not wear a glove on the right hand in order to make the wrist brace more clearly visible) so the line can slip easily through my hand as I bring the line in and let it out (Photo 2.11).

If your horse is very strong and you need to be able to really hold onto the line, however, gloves with rubber pimples on the fingers and palm will give you a better grip.

If you do a lot of longeing and ground driving, you might want to use wrist braces to give your wrists some support. This will help offset the stress of holding a whip (some are quite heavy) for long periods

of time and will support your wrist when you need to hold onto the line or give it a tug. In the photo (refer to Photo 2.11) you can see how the wrist brace fits under the glove.

If you know how to read the signs, your horse will tell you when he is warmed up, when he is ready to start new work, and when it is time to quit. If you tend to longe on and on and need to keep track of the time so you don't overwork your horse, or if your horse continually tries to convince you that it is time to quit, you'll need a watch to monitor the length of the session. I like a watch with a large face and real numbers so that, with a quick glance, I can see the time.

For safety and protection, keep your hair pinned, banded, or tucked out of the way. Hair should not interfere with your vision or concentration. Eyeglasses and sunglasses should be comfortable and fit securely. If you are constantly reaching up to reposition your glasses, you lose concentration and contact with the horse. Consider attaching an athletic band to the earpieces of your glasses to secure them at the back of your head.

If you wear a broad-brimmed hat, and you should, you can secure it on your head

2.12 *Protect yourself from the elements: broad brimmed hat with stampede string to secure it during wind, UV sunglasses, a snood or hairnet for long hair, long-sleeved shirt, neck bandanna, and gloves.*

with a stampede string (Photo 2.12). A stampede string attaches to the hat either by encircling the crown or fastening under the hatband. The string itself can be worn under the chin or at the back of the head. When it is snugged up, the wind or a sudden move will not dislodge your hat.

Although safety helmets are usually associated with riding, there are times when you are handling horses from the ground that it would be a good idea to wear one. If you are inexperienced or if you are working with a young, inexperienced horse, it would be to your benefit to wear a protective helmet. When you are working on a horse's legs, he could accidentally hit you in the head when he stomps at a fly, or he could move suddenly and knock you into a wall or a fence or onto the ground.

Sunscreen should be used to protect your skin from lesions that can result in skin cancer. Sun damage to skin is cumulative, beginning with childhood, so no matter what age you are, you should pay attention to this very real hazard of being a horse trainer. Sunburn can occur at any time of day during any weather or season, as 80 percent of UV rays go though clouds; and during the winter, 90 percent of the sun's rays are reflected off the snow. The UVB rays hit hardest, however, during the summer at high altitudes when the sun is the highest in the sky. Therefore, during those times, stay indoors or give yourself extra protection.

Always follow these rules:

- Wear gloves and a tight-weave, broad-brimmed hat.

- Wear sunglasses with UV protection.

- Whenever possible wear long-sleeved shirts with collars. Choose a shirt made of sun-proof materials.

- Use sunscreen on all exposed areas including face, neck, throat and upper chest, hands, and arms. Apply the lotion at least a half hour before exposure to the sun. Your skin should be dry so that the lotion can bond to your skin. Be generous and use a sunscreen with an SPF (sun protection factor) of at least 15. Use a lip product with an SPF of at least 15. Reapply all products after about two hours, or if you sweat. Some sunscreen products are available as a mist. Waterproof products can also be used. Wash and moisturize your skin after you come indoors.

- Consider wearing a bandanna around your neck, or turn up your shirt collar for further protection. The neck is one of the most common sites of melanomas.

- Try to stay indoors between 10 AM and 2 PM. Work your horse in the early morning and the late afternoon and evening, whenever possible.

3

OPENING THE LINES
OF COMMUNICATION

Learning to feel and to develop the use of your aids is essential *before* you begin to train a horse. For ground training, you need to create a set of reflex actions and body language "statements" that are smooth and consistent. The more physically fit and supple you are, the better able you will be to train a horse from the ground.

Understanding the composite effects of aids is more important than memorizing "sets of aids" or "cues" to get a horse to perform various maneuvers. Learn how to train by approaching it as a series of coordinated body movements rather than memorizing which buttons to push. For example, instead of thinking, "canter to trot," think "Settle my weight back on my heels, lower the whip, lower my eyes, say *'ta-rot'* with a falling inflection, and give a soft tug on the line," and you will likely find that your horse has made the transition from a canter to a trot. This way you see how your various body movements create various reactions in your horse. And in this way you can more accurately focus on which of your aids are working and which need development.

You influence a horse through the use of your natural aids and the employment of some artificial aids, when necessary. Your natural aids are your mind, your body, your arms, your legs, and your voice. Artificial aids are pieces of equipment that accent or augment your natural aids. Longe lines, whips, and all items of tack used on the head are considered artificial aids. Your aids and influences should not be applied in a haphazard manner.

- Aids should be fair and not contradictory. They should be applied humanely and in such a way that a horse can understand them in equine terms. Aids should not conflict, making it impossible for a horse to respond properly to one aid without being punished by another. In other words, don't whip and jerk at the same time.

- Aids should be appropriate. You could train a horse to stop when you blow a whistle, but that would be inconvenient and inappropriate. Following classic training guidelines is the best bet. That is why traditional equipment and aids are used in this book.

- Aids should be clear and direct. A horse does not reason, therefore you must make your signals to him a direct line of communication, not something he must figure out. Know the level of the horse's training so your aids will be delivered at an appropriate level for him.

- Aids should be consistent. Each time you want the horse to perform a particular maneuver, you should ask him in the same way he has been asked in the past. That is why consistent voice commands are so important.

- Aids should be precise and applied at the right moment, so that you make it easy for your horse to do the right thing. Your sense of timing will improve with practice, so it is best not to attempt a very complex maneuver until you are able to coordinate all the aids for it.

- Aids should be applied in the appropriate location. You must know horse reflexes and how a horse will react to stimuli applied to various areas of his body. If you were trying to get a horse to move his left shoulder to the right, it would make no sense to touch his hindquarters with the whip.

- Aids should be of optimum intensity. They should be applied strongly enough to be effective yet not too strong; otherwise they might frighten the horse or develop resistance in him. One of the goals of training is to get a horse to respond to lighter and lighter aids. When you need a greater response from your horse, don't automatically use a more forceful aid; instead, use a more effective aid. An abrupt, well-placed bump on the longe line rather than a steady pull will often get the response you want. Be firm, not hard or soft. Be effective.

  Use your aids lightly and increase them as needed. If a horse doesn't respond to a natural aid, you can use an artificial aid to reinforce it. Whether you use a natural aid or an artificial one, use it with only as much intensity as you can control. In other words, if you want your horse to move his shoulder away from you, apply the type and intensity of aid that will achieve a step sideways. It might be just fingertip pressure. If you press hard and lean into your horse, he may lean into you! Now you have one thing to correct and another thing to teach. You have created a worse situation by using too much force. You not only need to apply the aids with appropriate intensity, but you also need to be ready with counterbalancing aids (in this case, a hand on the lead rope/halter) to contain the horse's response and help to shape it into a desired form.

  The more responsive you make a horse to your aids, the lighter he will become because his body will develop a sense of forward motion and impulsion. If your driving aids are applied correctly, your horse will carry his head in a naturally pleasing configuration that does not have to be "held in position" with side reins but can instead be lightly guided into a more productive position.

- A reward for the horse (a release of the aids) should always follow as soon (within a second) as he responds correctly. This is sometimes tricky when you are using side reins because you hope the horse will reward himself by giving to himself and releasing pressure on the side reins. If you see that a horse never gets a "reward" but gets compact and tense, stop the session immediately and make adjustments. Sliding side reins (see Chapter 5, "Tack Tactics") allow the horse to more easily self-reward.

Aids vs Cues

There is a very important distinction between *aids* and *cues*. *Aids* are based on physical reflexes; *cues* are dependent on the horse's memory. An example of an aid is your pressing lightly on the horse's rib cage, which causes his body to curl (contract) around that pressure. This aid can be used in combination with various applications of other aids to develop many individual maneuvers, such as moving over while tied, turning on the forehand, side-passing, and so on.

Aids are based on a horse's reflex responses and initially the horse's reactions may be sudden and rough. Eventually, through desensitization and repetition, reflex responses can be tempered to an optimum intensity so the horse's body can be made to move correctly and with quality of movement as well.

Because reflexes are unconscious reactions, they can be a potential danger. A horse does not think before responding; he reacts automatically. For example, the bucking reaction to girth pressure can be a dangerous reflex. Fortunately, it is possible to override reflexes by training a horse to respond in more acceptable ways. In some cases, your goal will be to completely override a horse's reflexes; in other instances, you will want to dull his reflexes; and in certain situations, you will want to sharpen a horse's reflexes.

THE ROLE OF THE GROUND AIDS

AIDS	ROLE
Body movements	Both driving and restraining
Voice	Both driving and restraining
Whip	Mainly driving
Longe line and driving lines	Mainly restraining and shaping

The reflexes of the relaxed horse may be a tiny bit slower to respond to your aids than those of an excited horse, but a relaxed horse is also less likely to explode. Be aware that accidentally triggering a horse's reflexes can often result in a surprise and an accident.

A cue is a single signal for the horse to perform a particular maneuver. Cues are used in the training and performance of trick horses and are, in fact, part of your ground-training repertoire. For example, simply raising the longeing whip from horizontal to 30 degrees above horizontal is a cue for the trained horse to lope or canter. He has learned that association without an actual aid coming in contact with him.

Cues rely on the horse remembering a past association and a learned response. Therefore, cues are often the cause for anticipation. They are sometimes referred to as "buttons," magic signals that a trainer can use to tell a horse what to do. Because the horse either responds correctly to the cue or does not respond correctly, the trainer has little ability to affect the quality of the various parts of the response. That's why it is very important to be careful when making the association with your horse between a cue and the reaction that follows.

The Natural Aids

Your mind is a powerful force that helps you visualize, coordinate, evaluate, and modify all your training activities. Your voice is a human means of communication, yet one that is very appropriate for ground training.

Voice Commands

Along with body language, voice commands help you communicate with your horse. Carryovers from a horse's in-hand work to longeing and long lining are the voice commands for *walk, trot, whoa,* and *back.*

Voice commands will also be your link between longeing and riding. Since the body language you use during longeing won't carry over when you are in the saddle, it's nice to have a well-established set of voice commands to use during a horse's first lessons under saddle. Particularly useful for first rides are "Whoa," "Easy," and "Walk on," so be sure to make a strong connection with these helpful commands.

To be effective, a particular voice command should be consistent each time it is used. It should be consistent in tone, inflection, volume, and of course, in the word used.

Tone refers to the pitch of your voice, high and shrill or low and deep. It makes sense to use a higher-pitched voice to encourage a horse to move faster and a lower voice to slow him down or command him to stop.

Inflection is the way your voice modulates as you speak a word or phrase. It is the rise and fall or singsong quality of your voice. The emphasis given to a command can be crisp or drawling. A drawn-out command is soothing; a sharp command is a reprimand.

A high pitch and a great variation in inflection in "Ta-rot!" sounds as though you want the horse to move crisply forward.

A low pitch and a falling inflection with very little modulation variation, works well for "Whoa."

As for volume, it is neither necessary nor productive to shout commands at your horse because horses have a good sense of hearing. They can hear commands in quite low tones. In fact, the "breaking patter"

of experienced trainers is often just a muttering under the breath that human bystanders might not even be able to decipher but that the horse hears clearly.

The word that you choose to use for each voice command is really more significant for you than it is for the horse since you know what a word means, but to the horse it is just a particular sound. It is okay if you choose to use nontraditional words for your voice commands, but try to choose words that are very different from each other and that "sound" like what you want the horse to do. Decide ahead of time which words you will use as longeing commands and practice on a tape recorder until you perfect them.

Body Language

Since horses communicate with each other primarily by nonvocal means, we always need to be aware of what our body language is telling a horse.

Your body language can indicate confidence, strength, and specific expectations from a horse or it can show uncertainty, fear, or inattentiveness.

Your body movements alone can suddenly stop a horse, block him from

VOICE COMMANDS

"WALK ON!" with a higher pitch on "Walk" and great inflection variation; used to start a horse from a standstill.

"TA-ROT!" with a higher pitch on "Ta" and great inflection variation; used to trot a horse from a walk. When a horse is trotting, don't use the "Ta-rot" command. Instead, adjust the trot with "Easy" or "Trot on," as described later in this list.

"WAAAAAAALK" in a drawling, soothing tone to bring a horse down to a walk from a trot or canter.

"TRRRRAHHHHT" at a low pitch with little inflection variation; used to bring a horse down to a trot from a canter/lope.

"WHOA" An abrupt "Wo" with low pitch and punctuated end; used to promptly stop a horse from any gait. Not to be used in a soothing, drawling manner (that would be "Easy"). Here you want a prompt stop.

"EEEEE-ASY" A soothing, drawn-out middle tone command for slowing a horse down within a gait or generally just calming a horse.

"LET'S GO!" An energetic, brisk command (with accent and rising inflection on the "go!") for getting the horse to canter or lope. Many people use "Can-ter!"

"TROT ON" Very similar in sound to "Ta-rot," but spoken with more even inflection and in a more medium tone, designed to get a horse who is trotting in a lazy manner to trot forward with more energy.

"BAAAACK" Another soothing, drawn-out word in low, even tones, used during in-hand and long lining work to back a horse.

"TUUUURRRRRRRN" A melodic, circular command that starts out on a relatively high pitch and has a round, falling inflection. Used to change the horse's direction when free longeing or longeing on a line with a cavesson or halter.

"OKAY" Spoken just as though someone asked, "Would you hand me that bridle?" and you said, "Okay, I will." It's a prelude or "transition" command that I often use along with a half halt to let the horse know that something is coming and I don't want to surprise him. I use it with canter, "Okay, Let's Go!" and whoa, "Okay, Whoa."

"UH!" A staccato warning/reprimand noise that lets the horse know that you can see he is about to make a mistake, such as rushing at the trot and almost ready to break into a canter. This just gets the horse's attention focused more on you.

"GOOOOOD" ("GOOD BOY"/"GOOD GIRL") spoken with all the pleasure and pride you feel when your horse has done something particularly well. Use praise, but don't overuse it or it will lose its effect.

further movement, "open a door" for a horse to go through, make a horse gradually slow down and stop, or tell him to hurry up.

Because horses are basically followers, they are willing to accept guidance from you as long as you make your intentions clear and move with sure steps, smooth movements, and confidence.

Your body language includes your stance and demeanor, the size and intensity of your footsteps, the direction and intensity of your eyes, the position and movement of your arms.

When you approach a horse, before you "do" anything, the horse has already read your mood, expectations, state of health, and time schedule. All of this shows up in your overall stance and demeanor. If you march up to a horse briskly, with a very focused agenda and a time constraint, he might turn and move away from you. If, on the other hand, you mosey up to him as though you were just going to say "Hi," he'd likely stay put and greet you.

I rarely look a horse in the eye except when I am examining it for health purposes. Horses, like many animals, don't like strong, direct eye contact. They interpret it as a challenge, a stare-down. The more indirectly you look at a horse as you work with him, the more comfort-able he will be with whatever you are doing.

I've observed that trainers often give accidental, and often conflicting, cues without realizing it. For example, when free longeing, if the horse is tracking left and you are holding a whip in your right hand, you had better be aware of what your left hand is doing. If your left arm swings out to the side as you balance, you might (without realizing it) be asking the horse to slow down, stop, or even turn. Sometimes, as you are learning your tendencies, you might want to hold the non-active arm behind your back to keep it still until needed.

The Artifical Aids

The Whip

The whip is held in various positions to indicate to the horse the desired gait, speed, and length of stride (Drawing 3.0). Whip positions will vary slightly depending on the energy and training level of the horse. A lazy horse will need to see

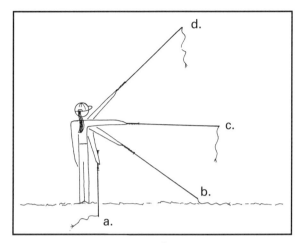

3.0   A. *Neutral position*
B. *Walk*
C. *Trot*
D. *Canter*

a dramatic change in the whip position when he is asked to canter, whereas an energetic horse will require very little signal. Some very alert, responsive horses need no whip signals because they are continually reading the trainer's body language.

Generally, the horizontal position is used for trot; a 30- to 45-degree elevation from that can be used for canter; and a position below the horizontal is used for walk. The whoa signal can be the whip touching the ground (out to your side), dropped on the ground, or held behind you.

Whip Talk

To add energy to the horse's movement, you can send jiggles or waves out to the end of the lash. To maintain the canter with a lazy horse, the whip can follow the horse by making rolling circles. To get a prompt response, you can pop the whip in the horse's direction.

If you feel you should contact the horse with the whip, popping him over the tail head with the lash of the whip generally causes a horse to drop his croup, which makes him move his hind legs forward and thus creates forward motion. But you must be close enough to the horse to hit your target accurately, otherwise you might get an unwanted response.

Whipping a horse's hindquarters or legs can cause a kick reflex, so work on your aim. Be sure a horse is at least 20 feet away from you before you attempt any encouragement with the whip.

Sometimes the whip is pointed at the horse's barrel to ask for more bend and to keep him out on the circle.

Practice coordinating your body language and your use of the whip.

CUELESS   The horse would be tracking left, free longeing. The whip in the right hand is lowered to the ground. The left arm is hidden behind the back to avoid inadvertent cueing (Photo 3.1). This is a neutral position and could be combined with other signals or voice commands to slow down or stop a horse.

3.2

3.3

3.1

ARM WHOA   With the whip dropped to the ground, taking a step toward the horse's forehand and putting the left arm out will slow or stop a horse and might turn a very reactive horse (Photo 3.2).

BUTT BLOCK   To emphasize the arm whoa, you can use the butt end of the longeing

whip as an extension that you can place in front of the horse's field of vision (Photo 3.3). This would also cause a horse to slow down, stop, or turn. If you place the entire length of the whip in front of the horse's vision, it has a much stronger effect.

TARGET PRACTICE   Tack a plastic yogurt container lid to your training pen rail and practice hitting it with the end of the lash of your whip (Photo 3.4). This will ensure that when you do want to contact your horse with the whip, your aim is good enough to deliver the whip tip to the spot you want so that you get the response you want.

3.4

The Longe Line

Talking on the Longe Line

Practice your longe line moves by attaching a line to your training pen rail.

MILD WAVE Sending a mild wave down the longe line usually causes the horse to slow down a notch. A "tremor" would be a milder vibration than that shown in this photo and would be used to get the horse's

attention back on his work (Photo 3.5). Pitching a "major wave" in the line, along with other body language and voice commands, is appropriate for telling the horse to perform a downward transition, for example, from a canter to a trot.

JERK A major backward jerk on the line is used to stop a horse suddenly, to gain

3.5

3.6

control of an unruly horse, or to stop a horse who has gone mindlessly into orbit. The jerk is most effective when it is preceded by a "lull," or a slackening in the line (Photo 3.6).

Getting a Grip on the Longe Line

Some longe lines have a loop on the end that is handy to hold when you're working a well-schooled horse on the end of a 35-foot line in a 70-foot circle. But holding a longe line by the loop on the end can be dangerous if your hand gets caught in the loop and the horse runs off. For reasons of safety, never hold the end loops. In fact, you could consider cutting the end loop so it cannot snag part of you.

When the horse is tracking left, hold in your left hand the portion of the longe line that is attached to the horse. The balance of the line, folded in a safe figure-eight, is held in your right hand. (Photo 3.7) If the horse were to suddenly bolt, the layers of the figure-eight would pull out of your hand without wrapping around your hand. But if instead the line were held in a coiled roll, when a horse bolted, the coil could tighten up very

suddenly and trap your hand. In this photo the left hand holds the line with a "feeling" grip, that is, the line enters the top of the hand, where the fingers can mete out the line and feel the contact. This is a sensitive but not definitive hold on the line. If the horse started to pull, it would be difficult to hold the line with the fingers.

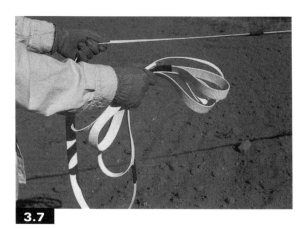

3.7

When the line passes up through the bottom of the hand, the line is held with a "control" grip (Photo 3.8). This is the most positive, secure hold on the line. The right angles the line makes through your hand create a more powerful hold with less effort.

When, while holding the line with a "control" grip, you want to "invite the horse to move more forward" (horse traveling

3.8

3.9

3.10

to the left), you merely rotate your hand 90 degrees to the right to unlock the hold, and then move your arm to the left to "lead him forward" (Photo 3.9).

If you would rather hold the longe line in one hand, here is the safest way to do so: "control" grip plus figure-eight plus end loop out of the way (Photo 3.10).

Here is one way to shorten the longe line while the horse is working: With the horse tracking left, the longe line is in your left hand and the whip is in your right. Run your right hand up the longe line a foot or two (Photo 3.11).

Then, as you bring the horse into a smaller circle, you pass the line you have

3.11

3.13

3.12

3.14

gathered to your left hand (Photo 3.12). The right hand then moves back to its driving position, holding only the whip.

Switching Hands on the Whip and Longe Line

When you want to change the direction your horse is working, you must change

the aids in your hands. The best way to avoid giving inadvertent cues to your horse is to change the whip behind your back.

When the horse is tracking left, the longe line is in your left hand and the whip is in your right hand, with your right hand facing forward. Rotate the whip in your right hand so the whip faces backward (Photo 3.13).

Next, reach behind your back and pass the whip from your right hand to your left hand (Photo 3.14).

You are now holding the whip, facing backward, and the longe line in your left hand. Bring your hands together in front of you. Simultaneously take the longe line in your right hand and rotate the whip in your left hand so it again faces forward.

Now you are set up for the horse to track to the right (Photo 3.15).

3.15

You can also change the whip in front of you. Although this might be more comfortable for you, it can confuse the horse because it might appear that you are giving him whip signals. So keep your whip low and quiet. Again, with the horse tracking left, the longe line is in your left hand and the whip is in your right (Photo 3.16).

To make the change, place the butt of the whip on top of the longe line and secure it with your left thumb while you reach for the longe line with the fingers of your right hand (Photo 3.17). Now you are ready to send the horse to the right.

3.16

3.17

It is possible to change the whip in front by passing the whip under the longe line loops, but depending on the size of the loops, this might be awkward. With the horse tracking left, longe line in left hand, whip in right, raise your left hand while at the same time passing the whip under the loops.

Open your left hand to accept the whip while holding the loops with your thumb and forefinger. Finish by taking the loops in your right hand.

Reading the Horse

To predict a horse's behavior you must know how to read horse body language. Be an astute, objective observer. Notice the details of body posture and action and learn what behaviors they precede. Here are some examples:

- *Acceptance.* See *Relaxed* and *Submissive*

- *Afraid.* Either shows characteristics of an excitable horse or "freezes" and has no reaction to any stimuli. Often tail is clamped.

- *Alert.* Listening, ears forward.

- *Angry.* Ears pinned, head extended and usually lowered, tail might be clamped or switching, often a red eye.

- *Belligerent/testy.* Large, bold movements, head high, muscles pumped up. Not listening.

- *Bored.* Not looking up or out, ears flaccid, head down.

- *Concentrating.* Ears usually tuned to trainer or slightly back.

- *Distracted.* Looking around, moving hindquarters from side to side, maybe pawing, either not responding or overreacting to the aids.

- *Dull.* Long reaction time with a low-intensity reaction.

- *Excited.* Swerving, swinging, pawing, whinnying, screaming, defecating, sweating, overreacting to the aids, tail held very high.

- *Irritated.* Ears flicking back and forth, tail swishing, picking up feet as if to kick.

- *Listening to trainer.* Ears pointed toward trainer. This might mean to the side when longeing, and could mean back when long lining from the rear.

- *Relaxed.* Head and neck held low and reaching, rhythmic breathing, back slightly arched and swinging, tail held off anus and swaying rhythmically with even tempo movement, contented snorting or blowing through nose, calm, inwardly focused eye.

- *Resistant.* Clenched jaw and mouth, tight muscles, head up, hollow back.

- *Silly.* Shaking head, sashaying back and forth, tail up high.

- *Sore.* Short, timid steps or very stiff movement, often with ears back.

- *Submissive.* "Clacking" in young horses (extended head with mouth working up and down as if chewing), chewing and working the tongue, head low.

- *Tired.* Uncoordinated, stumbling, inattentive to aids.

It is helpful to learn to read each individual horse. Pay attention to signs of exertion so you know when the horse is working hard. Is he grunting? Holding his ears at half-mast? You need to recognize when a horse is making an effort and when you can ask him for more. You need to know when you have gone past a horse's point of mental concentration or past the level of his physical condition. Pay close attention to the rhythm of his breathing, the movement of his ears, and the carriage of his tail.

When a horse does something other than what you have asked, you need to be able to determine whether he is, in effect, saying to you:

1. I am confused. I don't know what to do.

2. I am tired. My body is not ready to do this.

3. Do I have to? Can't I do this instead?

4. No. I don't have to obey you.

Some horses are selective listeners. They respond only to what they want to "hear." Say, for example, that you take a fresh horse out to free longe. He has been longed many times before. He immediately breaks into a fast trot and you say, "walk," and make sure that your whip is low and your motions are smooth as you move toward his head. There is no response from the horse—he just keeps trotting quickly. He acts as though he has never heard or seen this request. So you move the horse up to a lope for ten minutes to set it up for him to do the right thing. You take the edge off the horse's energy. You monitor the horse. You don't want to exhaust him, but you do want to get him to a point where he wants to stop. Then you ask him again for a walk, and lo and behold, he instantly melts into the ground at a soft walk. His "hearing" sure improved! A few such instances make a lasting impression on a horse.

Learning

Horses do not think things out ahead of time and plan their behavior. Horses act according to inherited instincts and precepts of behavior and react to a trainer's movements and touch with a deeply ingrained set of reflexes. A reflex is an automatic, unconscious response of a muscle (or a gland) to a stimulus.

Natural selection favored horses who escaped their predators because of highly developed instincts and reflexes. Horses are capable of quickly assuming thundering speeds from a standstill, of rising and running instantly from a lateral recumbent sleeping position, and of striking or kicking in the blink of an eye. These lightning-quick reflexes also allow today's horse to perform in a vast array of athletic events.

Horses are highly trainable because of their keen power of association and adaptability to our world. The horse's natural ability to link a stimulus (trainer's aid or cue) with a response (the horse's) makes the horse trainable. With an excellent memory, horses rarely forget experiences, whether good or bad. This benefits the experienced trainer because the horse remembers each well-designed lesson, and the trainer can build on the progression. The horse's excellent memory, however, can also work against less experienced trainers who might make mistakes with the horse. Each time a wrong response is learned, albeit inadvertently, it must be unlearned before a new response can be taught.

Once a horse has learned a lesson, anticipation can be troublesome. The horse might begin to act before any aids or cues are presented. He performs what he expects will be asked for. The horse's excellent memory and keen senses have allowed him to pick up signals from a particular place in the arena, the feel of a specific piece of tack, your body language, breathing, heartbeat, even your pheromones. All these are clues that he instantly pieces together and often reacts to before you even know you have cued him. This is the phenomenon that makes some people think horses are telepathic—they seem to read a human's mind. It is more likely that they are just keen observers with an excellent memory.

Although anticipation might seem harmless, if left unchecked, it can develop into a habit that makes a horse virtually uncontrollable. To prevent anticipation, vary the sequence of the lesson maneuvers and the location of the lessons, and keep things progressing forward. See *101 Longeing and Long Lining Exercises: English and Western* for exercise variations.

The first type of learning that a foal experiences is *imprinting*. This is the process of dam and foal bonding that takes place during the first few hours after birth. The smells and the quiet nickering exchanged between foal and dam link the two together. The foal receives from the mare various types of horse communication that encourage and help him develop his innate horse behaviors and reflexes. Once the species bond has been firmly established between mare and foal, usually by the second day, human familiarization can begin. Premature interference can cause confusion.

The foal learns much by mimicking the behavior of its dam as well as that of other horses. When a mare takes a foal across the creek for the first time, the foal goes through the water because the mare does, and the foal just follows along. Young horses are observant and curious and always watching and learning. I've often observed weanlings, yearlings, and two-year-olds who are turned out in a pasture adjacent to my training pen and arena. They come as close as they can to the round pen or arena and watch what I am doing with another horse. They stand for long periods of time and appear to be studying intently. It doesn't surprise me, then, that when it comes time for a young horse to be trained, he takes to it easily because he has long observed other horses being trained.

Behavior

Through *behavior modification* you influence and develop your horse's natural behaviors and reactions into a useful format. When a horse acts according to your desires, and you want to encourage him to repeat such behavior in the future, you need to reinforce that behavior. When his behavior is undesirable, you need to indicate to him that it is undesirable by discouraging the behavior. Then you must show him a different way to act and reward him when he exhibits the new behavior.

There are four ways to modify a horse's behavior: positive reinforcement, negative reinforcement, punishment, and extinction. Positive and negative reinforcement encourage a behavior. Punishment and extinction discourage a behavior.

Positive Reinforcement

Rewarding a horse for good behavior by giving him something pleasant following the desirable behavior is reward or *positive reinforcement*. This encourages the horse to repeat the behavior in the future. Although not always handy for routine training situations, a food treat is interpreted by the horse as a reward.

Rest after working hard is also inherently interpreted as a reward, but it has limited application. If a horse were full of vim, a rest break would not be a reward; it would be a restriction. But if a horse has been cantering on the line in side reins and you stop him, walk over to him and loosen the lines, and let him stand and catch his breath or walk on a long rein, he interprets that as a reward for a job well done.

Fortunately, horses can also be conditioned to appreciate other actions as rewards. A word of praise or a soothing pat on the neck can also tell a horse he has done something correctly. These kinds of positive reinforcers are often most convenient for everyday horse training.

The demands of training often require intense concentration and physical exertion on the part of a horse. That's why it is important to periodically reward him during the lessons to keep his mental attitude fresh and enable his body to respond properly. A reward not only tells a horse he is doing well, but it also builds his confidence and adds to his enjoyment of the work. It is not feasible for you to elaborately reward a horse after each properly performed movement, yet there are ways to assure a horse that he is working well.

Many trainers fit into one of two categories when it comes to doling out rewards. Some who are quick to use punishment to correct a horse take the same horse's good behavior for granted and are sparse with rewards. This may be caused in part by reluctance to "not make a move" when the horse is working correctly, or it may be due to a philosophy that the horse should continue along unless the trainer tells him to do things differently.

Other trainers may attempt to use reward to soothe or bribe a horse into good behavior, or may lavish rewards on a horse with such intensity and frequency that the reward no longer has a productive effect on the horse. The horse cannot sort out exactly which behavior is being reinforced and which behavior to continue. Some horses can come to expect and even demand reward for just about any behavior. So, to be most effective, a trainer must understand how reinforcement works and find a middle ground.

Negative Reinforcement

Removing a negative stimulus after a horse has performed a desired behavior is termed *negative reinforcement*. When you are teaching a young horse to move forward on the longe line, a tap with the whip on the croup or hindquarters tells him, via his natural reflexes, to move forward. The negative stimulus stops as soon as the horse moves forward. Each time it will take less application of the negative stimulus, the whip, to get the horse to move forward. Soon just the visual cue of a raised whip will elicit the correct response. The horse has been trained, by negative reinforcement, to recognize a cue.

Application of Positive and Negative Reinforcers

Both positive and negative reinforcement are designed to encourage a particular behavior in the future. Together they can be thought of as *reinforcers*—actions by a trainer to encourage desirable behavior. Whether you use positive or negative reinforcers, they should be immediate, consistent, appropriate, and brief. A good trainer is an objective observer, only noting *actual* behaviors, not *interpreting* a horse's actions.

Things that a horse inherently perceives as either positive or negative are *primary* reinforcers. Examples of positive primary reinforcers (rewards) are food, a scratch on the withers, a rest break; negative primary reinforcers are pressure on the mouth and a tap with the whip. The horse does not have to be taught to feel good about positive primary reinforcers or bad about negative primary reinforcers—his reaction to them is intrinsic.

Secondary reinforcers must be learned. Positive secondary reinforcers are things the horse learns to appreciate, such as a kind word. To teach a horse to perceive a secondary reinforcer as a reward, you should link it initially with a positive primary reinforcer. For a horse to respond to the trainer's voice as a reward, consistent words, tone, and inflection must be used at times when the horse is receiving a primary reinforcer. For example, if you were to say, "Good Boy!" in a pleasant, praising voice as you fed your horse a treat or gave him a scratch on the withers, when you later used the phrase during an active training situation, it would tend to elicit a sense of contentment in the horse and he would likely relax and stretch.

Negative secondary reinforcers are not really clear-cut in horse training. They tend to be based on warnings or a horse's anticipation of something negative coming. For example, say that a horse is supposed to stand still on the longe line until asked to move forward. The trainer sees that the horse's attention is wandering and makes a warning noise like a deep "uh-uh." This sound can help the horse regain his concentration because he anticipates that if he moves, he will receive pressure on his nose from a tug on the longe line. Here, a gruff warning could be thought of as a negative secondary reinforcer. A verbal scolding after the fact, however, would technically be classified as punishment, which is discussed later.

Using Rewards

For a secondary reinforcer to retain its conditioned effect, you must periodically refresh the horse's memory by linking primary pleasurable experiences with it. Using a variety of primary reinforcers (rest, scratching, feed) will make a stronger, more long-lasting connection. If you use a secondary reinforcer too often ("Good Boy" at every step) or without periodic substantiation, it may lose its effect. The overused reinforcer may no longer represent contentment to a horse and it can lose its importance to him.

It takes a trainer with good knowledge, a keen sense of feel, and good reactions to reward a horse properly and effectively. The young or inexperienced horse must be rewarded even though his awkward attempts are far from the ideal. The experienced trainer will recognize the successive approximations to the eventual desired behavior and will assure the horse all throughout training that he is on the right track, so to speak. A trainer whose experience is only with advanced horses might find it difficult to recognize subtle progress in a young horse's attempts and fail to reward him.

For a reward to bring optimum results, it must occur immediately after the behavior it is reinforcing, it must appear consistently each time the behavior appears (at least at first), it must be of the proper intensity and duration, and it must be a reward appropriate to the type of work and the temperament of the individual horse.

Food is a very appropriate reward to teach a horse to come and be caught or to stand still when turned loose. If food were used as a reward during groundwork such as longeing and long reining, however, it would encourage the young horse to come into the center of the circle toward the trainer. Treats given at nonspecific times can show a horse that you are generally pleased with him. Although it may improve his interest in you, it will likely teach him to be pushy, to nibble, and to be disrespectful of your space.

During a ground-training session, there are several effective ways to show a horse he is doing well. Many horses respond positively to a hand on the withers or a soothing touch on the forehead. This stems partly from the innate social behavior of mutual grooming in which two horses demonstrate their bonding by massaging each other along the spine and rubbing their heads on each other. Simply letting your hand rest on the withers or giving a few soothing strokes to the forehead relaxes and softens most horses into lowering the neck and reaching forward, which is a sign of contentment and well-being.

I have seen some trainers deliver a loud slap to the horse's shoulder or ribs when a horse has done particularly well. To me, that hardly seems something a horse would naturally enjoy. Yet I've observed horses who appear to tolerate it, or perhaps they have just learned to associate it with the rest break which usually accompanies the slap. One way to determine what type of touch reward your horse inherently prefers is to turn him loose in a stall or small pen and try a long, smooth stroke on the neck, a scratch with the fingers on the withers, a slap on the neck, and a flat clap on the flank. He will clearly show you which he intrinsically interprets as a gift.

Another way to reward during a training session is to let the horse rest and fill up on air after he has worked hard. This does not mean cantering for hours and then letting him collapse in a heap on the rail. Periodically allow the horse to walk on light contact or stand quietly for a minute. Rest and stretching into long or loose side reins also reinforces the immediately preceding work and should be interspersed in the lessons, especially lessons that require collection.

The Yield as Reward

The release of pressure, or yielding to the horse, when he is performing properly is the reinforcement cornerstone in dressage work and classical Western training and should be regularly implemented in the training of any horse. *Yielding* means a softening of the active aid, not a giving away of what has been gained. Yet this principle is very difficult to apply to longeing when side reins are fixed. When you get to long lining, you will have a better opportunity to yield.

Normally, a certain degree of yielding should occur at each instance of compliance. If done correctly, this results in such frequent softening that there is little chance you will become stiff or try to hold your horse in position.

The more you learn to yield each time a horse makes a positive action, the more you will encourage the horse to develop a sense of self-carriage. He will develop the notion of using his body in balance, based on his own motivation, without depending on the aids to hold him together. It is somewhat of an honor system: You give the horse a little slack, so to speak, and see what he does with it. Does he fall on his forehand terribly, or fling his head up, or let his shoulder bulge out? Or does he hold himself together in a soft and balanced frame as though invisible forces were guiding him. A young horse will only be able to show you self-carriage for a few steps or so at a time. This is something that will gradually develop in the young horse. If you or your horse become dependent on side reins, self-carriage will never be fully developed. Side reins are meant to be a stepping stone in the training progression.

Sometimes the restraining forces of the longe line or driving lines must be used to an explicit degree to keep a horse from "running through," or ignoring the aids. But once the horse complies, there must be a yielding. If you prod a horse constantly with the whip, yet hold him rigidly with the lines without a letup, the horse has no means, no incentive to learn compliance. The trainer who does not reinforce a horse's good movement with a softening teaches the horse to become very tough or to look for an explosive way to evade the relentless aids.

Punishment

When you administer something unpleasant to a horse to discourage a certain behavior, you are punishing him. Sometimes all that is necessary is a verbal reprimand, but often physical discipline is needed to make a lasting impression on a horse. If a horse refuses to stop when you are leading him, you may have to resort to a chain over his nose, so when he tries to run over you, you can apply pressure on the chain to discourage that from (re)occurring. As the horse is disciplined with the chain, a voice command ("Whoa") should be used

simultaneously, so eventually the voice command alone will produce the same results. The same applies to work on the longe line, although horses who have good in-hand lessons rarely have to be punished on the longe line.

Always use the least amount of force or punishment necessary to get the job done. Starting out at a low intensity leaves you room to increase the intensity, as necessary, and ensures that the horse is being treated fairly and humanely. It is also important to be assertive enough to successfully complete the job, however. Continual "nagging" by ineffectively tugging on a lead rope can serve not only to develop resentment in a horse but also to desensitize him to the use of future low-level stimuli.

Punishment must be administered immediately, otherwise a different behavior might be punished. A subjective rule of thumb is that for punishment to be effective, the reprimand must be delivered within one to two seconds after the undesirable behavior occurs. If a horse takes off with a lurch and a swish of a tail when you first let him out on the longe line, and you are caught off guard and just let him take off at a trot or canter, he has been rewarded for a bad behavior.

Your inclination might be to not do anything and "let the horse burn off energy," which would further reinforce the bad behavior. Or you might think that you should bring the horse back in and punish him right then and there, but if you did, you would be teaching the horse to be afraid of you approaching him. So what you must do is bring the horse in, reward him with a pat for coming in, and then be ever vigilant as you prepare to send him out on the longe line again. In fact, set the stage for him to repeat the bad behavior by repeating whatever set him off. But this time, be prepared to hold the horse close so you can deliver a good tug on the noseband of the cavesson. Then say, "Walk," walk a few steps with him, and then stop. Feign sending him out several more times until you feel he has given up the attempts at bad behavior and realizes you still have control. Then actually send him out, but bring him right back in, repeating this several times until you know he has the idea of proper behavior.

Extinction

Extinction is the removal of something pleasant to discourage the behavior it follows. If you turn a horse loose in a round pen to free-longe him and he just takes off and flat races around the pen ignoring you, instead of waiting until he tires himself out, you can use extinction to discourage his runaway behavior. You do this by taking away his freedom, by repeatedly stepping in front of him and making him turn. Usually after about four or five turns, the runaway behavior disappears because the horse's freedom has been removed. With extinction, however, the animal's undesirable behavior often becomes greatly amplified and embellished before it diminishes—things get worse before they get better. The horse will turn very quickly and frantically, jumping out into a dead run in the opposite direction, often getting ahead of the trainer and sometimes crashing into the rails of the pen. Understandably, this is when many people might relax their pressure and give in and let the horse run around the pen, but it is precisely the time when the behavior is about to change. After a few hard turns, the horse will look for a different way to behave.

If a horse has learned that when he speeds up, his inexperienced trainer will remove all demands, the horse has learned that he can get something good (freedom and absence of demands) by speeding up. When a capable trainer confronts the horse about this habit, the trainer is using the principle of extinction to change the horse's behavior. The trainer no longer allows the horse to have the feeling of freedom but instead controls the horse with aids. As expected, things will get worse before they get better. The horse will try frantically to push through the aids because in the past he was successful at achieving the pleasant state of not having to be restricted. But the persistent, capable trainer perseveres, and as soon as the horse submits by changing his focus and thinking of another way to behave, the trainer backs off a little. Once the horse has initially submitted, each subsequent time the capable trainer holds the aids on the horse, it will take less and less time for the horse to soften. Soon the horse will be retrained by extinction and will automatically have a soft and relaxed movement upon application of the aids.

Shaping

Once a horse has a pretty strong notion of what he should or should not do in response to a particular set of aids, you should begin to ask for gradual improvement in *form*. This is called *shaping*, or reinforcing successive approximations to a desired behavior.

When first teaching a canter depart, you might settle for any type of depart as long as it doesn't include bucking or running away. You begin to hone the transition until the horse not only canters on the correct lead from a trot or a walk, but also does so with proper balance, rhythm, and engagement. Getting to that stage is a series of steps that spans many lessons. The horse must be rewarded each time he gets closer to the eventual goal.

Remember the following principles as you shape your horse's behavior:

- *Pick the best base to begin with.* In the preceding example, it would make sense to the horse if the first time you asked for canter, you were in a familiar longeing pen and used progressive voice commands and body language based on his previous work. It's best to start on a solid, familiar base.

- *Reward all approximations to the desired behavior.* If a horse bolts into a canter, you should not punish and can even praise the horse for his attempt. Be especially careful not to bump the horse's head or mouth as he would interpret this as punishment for cantering. Even if a young horse takes the wrong lead, it is usually best to reward him for at least cantering, before you try again for a particular lead. Soon the horse will relax, respond to your positioning aids, and the correct response will come easily.

- *Don't go too fast toward the goal.* If you try to reach perfection in just a few lessons, the horse may be missing valuable connections between the maneuver's components. If you expect a balanced, collected canter too early, you may lose forward motion and cause your horse to get bunched up or behind the bit. The beauty of following a systematic training scheme is that when you have problems, you always have a progression that can be reviewed.

- *Don't get stuck in one particular stage.* If you are three-quarters of the way to the ultimate goal but you no longer gear the lessons for forward progress, it will likely be more difficult to move the horse on to a more advanced behavior. If during the latter stages of initial training, the horse is allowed six or seven trot strides in between a transition from walk to canter, it may be more difficult to suddenly eliminate them all than to systematically decrease their number. Keeping the lessons moving in a progressive fashion will yield maximum performance and satisfaction.

Customize Your Training Program

Although training books, by design, must be written in somewhat of a step-by-step format, horses do not always learn things in a linear fashion. That is, once you get past the first few lessons, you may find that there is no longer a strict order to the lessons. Also, at various times you will recognize the need to ride up on a plateau for a period, repeating and reinforcing exercises before bringing in something new. There will also be times when you will emphasize a previous lesson.

When do you push and when do you quit? In contrast to some aspects of ground training (in-hand, tying, restraint), very few lessons involved with longeing and ground driving are black or white and need to be resolved with absolutes. In other words, you rarely should need to bring something to issue during this aspect of training. If you feel that you need to confront a horse, it may be an indication that the in-hand and barn manners are not sufficient.

That being said, there are times when it is advantageous to push a horse:

- There are times in a horse's training when things get worse just before a breakthrough. If you know your horse and know horse training principles, a push here is better than giving up just when things are at their worst.

- Another time you might want to push your horse is when you have done all the prep work, yet he does not respond properly. When the horse has tried "everything" but the right response, pushing him just a bit more might help him discover another way of responding.

Knowing when to quit is one of the most important things a horse trainer can learn:

- Quit when the session is an "accident looking for a place to happen."

- Quit when you are hot, flushed, angry, or too tired to work well.

- Quit when a horse repeatedly gives the "wrong" response. Don't keep repeating what you are asking because, obviously, it is not working. You will need to change something, find a new way, perhaps on a new day, to communicate with your horse.

- Quit when your horse is nearing the bottom of his physical reserve, is not paying attention, or is behaving in a dangerous manner. Pushing might not serve a productive purpose and might undermine other positive things you have established. If a horse is exhausted, he might hurt himself, tune out completely, and learn something worse than what you are trying to correct.

- Quit when things are going well for a moment, even though you may or may not have accomplished the overall goal of the session. Sometimes it is better to quit on a good note before it is "too late."

Most of the time, it is best to work for gradual progress rather than an all or nothing reaction. Use patience and planning to make, not break your horse.

Safety

Handling young horses can be risky. Because of the nature of the equipment used in ground training, your vulnerability, and the unpredictable outbursts characteristic of untrained horses, things can get confusing and dangerous.

By practicing safe horse handling and training practices you will greatly minimize your chances of accidents when working with a horse. Most horse-related mishaps are caused by one of the following:

- A lack of understanding in reading horse body language; lack of experience handling horses; lack of ability, not having a way with horses.

- Carelessness, lack of attention, and overconfidence.

- Working in unsafe facilities.

- Inadequate or improper training of the horse.

- Inadequate or improper training and/or supervision of the handler or trainer.

- Unsuitable horse.

- Equipment failure.

- Poor equipment fit.

- Bad luck, such as horse spooks, slips, or falls.

- Handler or trainer hasn't planned for emergencies.

- Loss of temper.

- Presence of other horses and distractions.

Shortcutting proper safety practices is probably the number-one cause of equine-related accidents. Don't attempt to teach a horse something that is beyond your capabilities and don't attempt a maneuver that is far too advanced for a particular horse. Keep the pace of your training schedule conservative and steady.

Commonly, when a horse is faced with a lesson that he is unable to accept or resolve, he reacts with some sort of undesirable avoidance behavior. Rushed training can cause explosive reactions such as bucking, rearing, or running away as well as chronic and sometimes insidious attitudes such as sullenness, uncooperativeness, and boredom.

Because of their size, strength, and quick reflexes, all horses are potentially dangerous. A horse's power and unpredictability are often underestimated and can surface unexpectedly, especially when the horse is being presented with something new.

As a safeguard, always carry a sharp pocketknife in case the only way out of a dilemma is to cut ropes or other tack. Even though quick-release knots and panic snaps are often used, there are times when the weight of a struggling horse can prevent these safety devices from operating.

Because so many ground-training procedures involve ropes and long lines, you should become accustomed to wearing gloves for protection against rope burn. Never wrap or loop a rope around your hand, arm, or any other part of your body. Wear boots or appropriate shoes to protect yourself from the frequent missteps a young horse makes as he gains balance and confidence.

Only use equipment of the strongest type and periodically inspect it for wear so the young horse will not learn bad habits. If a horse escapes by breaking a piece of weak equipment, he can set the stage for a life-long bad habit of attempting to repeat the behavior.

Tack should be well stitched and constructed from durable materials that are not fatigued from long use, sweat, dirt,

sun, or rain. Hardware should be of the highest-quality material and workmanship. Don't use tack that is merely attractive; be sure it will be reliable under severe stress. Make dependability, not cost, your number-one priority when choosing training tack.

Safe Practices

Groundwork holds several dangerous elements. One is being kicked. Horses can kick with one or both hind legs out to the side as well as behind, and any kind of kick is dangerous. Therefore, at all times, be aware of the range of the hind legs and work in a safe position.

It is rare, but horses sometimes strike with their front legs at unfamiliar items on their heads. So when you put a bridle or cavesson on your horse for the first time, just be aware of this possible reaction.

Horses usually buck or hump their backs and jump forward the first time they feel girth pressure. That's why it's a good idea to hold the first lesson involving a surcingle or saddle in a training pen rather than in the crossties of the barn. Be aware that even if a horse stands perfectly still to be saddled the first time, when you ask him to take that first step, he is likely to at least crow-hop a bit.

Hold the longe line safely, as previously described. Keep an upright but hinged "warrior" posture: shoulders and head back, hip and knee joints slightly flexed, upper arms at your side with elbows bent. If you lean your upper body forward or reach out with your arms, you have lost your stability. Of course, for momentary giving, such as with an upward transition, you can reach out a bit for just a few seconds. If your horse is tracking along rhythmically and in balance, your feet will be next to each other, more or less pivoting in a small circle at the center of the longe circle.

If your horse is pulling, however, your right leg (if your horse is going left) should be well weighted and positioned behind your left leg for added control. If a horse is hesitant to move forward on the line to the left, for example, your right foot should be stepping forward with encouraging body language. For more on body language and communication, see the next chapter.

4

IN-HAND WORK
A HORSE IN THE HAND IS
WORTH TWO ON THE LOOSE

Too often in-hand work is merely a means to an end rather than a specific goal itself. It is "getting a horse from point A to point B." The horse is coaxed with grain or cornered; there is a bit of a wrestling match as the halter is put on; the horse drags the person to the tack and grooming area; then it's a hit-and-miss affair on the way to the arena where the bad in-hand manners carry over to the longeing, long lining, or riding.

Whether you are working with an untrained horse or trying to improve the manners of an older horse, start from square one and spend plenty of time on in-hand lessons. They will help you immeasurably in the upcoming basic longeing lessons and are the basis for all training to come. Give special attention to tack selection and fit, consistency, position, and safety.

Tack

When choosing a halter for in-hand work, choose one that buckles easily, fits well, and is strong. The noseband of a properly fitted halter should rest one to two fingers below the prominent cheekbone. The crownpiece should rest just behind the ears, not slip down the horse's neck. The throatlatch should fit in the horse's throatlatch. (Photo 4.1)

4.1

If a halter is buckled too low on a horse's nose, the noseband lies on the fragile tip of the nasal bone, which could become fractured if too much pressure were exerted. If a halter is too large, it will be ineffective, and as it moves around the horse's face, it could injure the horse's eyes (Photo 4.2). If a halter is too tight or small, it puts constant pressure on the horse's nose and poll. This is uncomfortable for the horse and can "deaden" the tissues where there is pressure, resulting in a loss of response to cues.

4.2

Leather halters are fine for in-hand work but may not be strong enough for tying. Nylon web halters are the best for in-hand and tying.

An ideal lead rope for in-hand work is 10 to 12 feet (finished length). Use 5/8-inch cotton rope back-spliced at one end and with a nonrusting heavy-duty snap spliced into the other end. All splices should be whipped with cotton cord. Cotton is a soft, natural fiber. Because it is the least abrasive of lead rope materials, it tends to deliver fewer rope burns than other types of rope. The downside is that cotton rope tends to fray. To prevent this and extend the life of your cotton ropes, keep them clean and dry.

Round nylon rope is strong, resistant to the damaging effects of moisture, and comes in pretty colors. It is not as secure to hold onto as cotton. Wear gloves when handling any rope, especially nylon.

4.3

Position

Hold the lead rope 6 to 8 inches from the snap (Photo 4.3). To adjust the distance between your hand and the halter, you can let the rope slide out through your fingers and take up slack by walking your fingers up the rope. Fold the excess lead rope in a figure-eight and hold it in your other hand, making sure you have no fingers inside the loops of the eight. Then, if the horse suddenly lurches forward, the rope will slide cleanly out of your hand one loop at a time. Be careful if you hold the excess lead rope in a circular coil because your hand could become trapped inside the coil if the horse suddenly bolted.

Stay in position between the horse's head and his shoulder, about an arm's length away. If you use a longer lead, the horse could turn his forehand away from you and his hindquarters toward you. A shorter hold, and you are asking to be stepped on or crowded. Keep your focus forward, alert, yet aware of what the horse is doing at all times.

If you are working with a young horse or one who constantly charges forward, be sure you hold the rope so that it comes in the bottom of your hand and out the top because this gives you the most "whoa power."

Whenever you handle ropes that are connected to horses, be sure to always wear leather gloves to protect your hands from rope burns and to give you a better grip on the rope.

Carry a 30- to 40-inch whip in the same hand as the excess lead rope. Hold the whip at mid-handle for the best balance. If you don't have an in-hand whip, you can use your longe whip with the lash spiraled around the shaft and tied above the handle.

If your horse starts to crowd you when you are leading (this is often a sign of insecurity), tell him to keep his distance by bumping the side of his neck with your elbow (refer to Photo 4.3).

For safety, always turn the horse away from you. When leading the horse from the near side, turn the horse to the right. While you are reviewing and fine-tuning in-hand work, make a strong, consistent association with voice commands so your in-hand review will carry over and benefit you and your horse when it comes time to introduce longeing.

Forward Movement

To encourage forward movement, *never* pull on the lead rope to try urging the horse forward. When leading at the walk, move forward energetically as though you have somewhere to go. Look ahead. Maintain a position at the midpoint of the horse's neck, between his head and shoulder. If the horse lags, encouragement should come from behind in the form of a light tap on the rump from a whip. Strive to stay in proper position at the horse's shoulder. When the horse is moving ahead calmly, there should be no pressure on the halter or any contact from the whip.

Trot in Hand

When leading at a trot, maintain your position at the midpoint of the horse's neck. Be sure you are holding the lead rope 6 to 10 inches from the snap so the horse has room to trot up. Ask the horse to begin trotting at the same time by whatever means you customarily use: "Ta-rot!," or a *click-click* sound with your tongue against your teeth, or a light tap with the whip on his hindquarters.

Now that you have reviewed basic leading, introduce the idea of performing the same maneuvers but on the end of a much longer lead. With the horse 3 to 4 feet away from you, walk and trot in-hand. This will get him used to the upcoming idea of longeing.

Although it is customary to regularly handle horses from the near (left) side, all horses should also be handled from the off (right) side. Any awkwardness on your part should be overcome through practice with a trained horse before you try offside maneuvers with an untrained horse.

Be sure that you practice every exercise in this book from both the near and off side of the horse. This will help prevent you and your horse from developing one-sidedness, and when it comes time to send your horse off to the right on the longe line, you will be very glad you worked him from the off side!

Slow Down or Stop

If the horse charges ahead, give a couple of light tugs on the lead rope. If he is really charging ahead, turn him to the right, into the fence, to slow him down. To slow down or stop some older untrained horses, you may need to use a visual barrier, such as the handle of the whip appearing in front of the horse's face at the same time the more normal aids are being applied. A chain over the nose is another option to gain control and prevent injury.

Gaining Control of the Horse's Head

If you can control a horse's head, you can control the horse. If you can't handle a horse's head, you won't be able to halter,

bridle, or guide him. To review head control, stand on the near side. Place your left hand on the bridge of his nose and apply light fingertip pressure to his poll (Photo 4.4). This should cause him to lower his head.

Now review lateral flexion. Standing on the near side place your left hand on the right side of the bridge of the horse's

4.4

nose and apply light pressure to bring his head to the left, toward you (Photo 4.5). The horse should comply softly and without raising his head. Reverse the aids and perform the exercise from the off side (Photo 4.6).

4.5

4.6

Although it should not be necessary for routine training, sometimes a chain, used in conjunction with a well-fitting halter, will help you gain control of an unruly or headstrong horse during in-hand work. It should not be substituted for a thorough training program, but it can give you a mechanical advantage over an unruly animal. Properly applied and used, a chain can prevent a horse and handler from getting hurt. A chain should be used with intermittent pressure and release, *not* steady pulling or pressure. *A horse should never be tied with a chain.*

Simply snapping a chain shank to the halter ring under the jaw of the horse serves no purpose other than to force you to hold onto an uncomfortable chain. It is not recommended for any situation.

A chain threaded through the halter, under a horse's jaw, encourages the horse to raise his head when the lead rope is pulled. A sleepy horse who needs to pay attention in halter classes, for example, might benefit from this chain setup. Otherwise, it is not the most effective means for getting a horse under control.

A chain over the horse's nose is the most common and useful means of restraint. The horse should be held with halter and lead rope while the chain is attached. Pass the snap up through the throat ring and then through the near cheek ring from outside to inside. Cross the chain over the noseband of the halter. This will prevent the chain from slipping down on the horse's nose when pressure is released. Pass the snap up through the far cheek ring from inside to outside. Attach the snap to the upper halter ring. Alternatively, you can run the chain from the far cheek ring back down to the throat ring of the halter and snap the chain to itself, thus making a loop around the horse's nose. Attach the lead rope snap to the chain. Using a chain in either manner prevents the chain from slipping down to the sensitive cartilage of the horse's nose and keeps halter twisting to a minimum. Chain use is appropriate for in-hand work only, not for tying or longeing.

The first time a chain is used on a horse, the horse might rear or strike, so caution is in order. Often only one or two lessons are necessary to teach a horse better in-hand manners. You should then be able to remove the chain and work successfully with just a halter. A chain is best reserved for use on horses one year or older and by someone experienced with horse training

and restraint. Chains are usually not necessary if a horse has had proper early handling.

"Whoa" on the Long Line

Whether for show, photography, or just good manners, all young horses should be taught to stand still on the end of a 10-foot lead rope (Photo 4.7). Make a strong connection in the horse's mind with the voice command "Whoa." This is essential and invaluable when you begin longeing and long lining. Even though you leave your usual position at the horse's shoulder, the horse should learn that he is supposed to stand still. At first, asking a young horse to stand for five or ten seconds is adequate.

4.7

4.8

4.9

Gradually build up a horse's patience so he will stand for several minutes without moving a foot.

Once the horse has the idea, move in a 360-degree circle around the horse, at the end of the 10-foot line. Step directly in front of the horse and make sure you stand in the horse's blind spots at his hindquarters on both sides (Photo 4.8). Whenever you think he requires a verbal reminder, use your voice command, "Whoa."

Turn on the Hindquarters

To perform the maneuver, shift the horse's weight back to the hindquarters with light pressure on the halter's noseband. At the same time, shift the weight of the horse from the left to the right side by pushing the lead rope under the horse's neck to the right and slightly backward. From a halt, move your right hand under the horse's neck to the off side (Photo 4.9). If necessary you can intermittently press the butt end of the longe whip or the fingers of your left hand on the side of the horse's shoulder. If the horse tends to leap forward, a little backward pressure on the halter will encourage him to settle his weight rearward for the turn.

The elements of the turn on the hindquarters should be reviewed. You will be performing the turn on the hindquarters when you ask your horse to turn during free longeing. When it comes time for long lining, you will teach him the walk-around turn on the hindquarters with long reins. If he has a very solid connection with the maneuver during in-hand work, the longeing and long lining will come much easier.

The front feet step a half circle around the hindquarters, specifically the hind pivot foot or pivot point. In a turn to the right, for example, (refer to Photo 4.9) the pivot foot is the right hind. It should bear most of the horse's weight in the turn, and it is relatively stationary and directly underneath the horse. The left hind walks a tiny half circle around the right hind. The left front leg crosses over and in front of the right front leg, and then the right front steps out to the side again. This is repeated as the front legs move in a semicircle.

The turn to the left must be performed from the off side of the horse, and the footfall patterns and aids are reversed.

Turn on the Forehand

When a horse is taught to move over while tied, he is learning a rudimentary form of the turn on the forehand. And he is being taught the important safety and positioning lesson you will need during longeing and ground driving: "Move your hindquarters away from me!"

In the turn on the forehand, the hind legs step a half circle around the stationary forehand of the horse. More specifically, if the hindquarters are moving to the right, or away from you if you are standing on the near side, the horse is walking around his left front leg.

In order to weight the pivot point in this turn to the left, turn the horse's head and neck slightly toward the left front leg. This lightens up the right forefoot and allows it to step its small circle around the relatively stationary left front foot. To activate the hindquarters in their larger semicircle to the right, apply pressure at the ribs, on the left side (where your leg will later be positioned when you ride).

To perform a turn on the forehand left, hindquarters moving to the right, stand on the near side and tip your horse's nose to the left, slightly toward you, to weight the left front leg (Photo 4.10). Then cue him on the left side with very light intermittent pressure to cause him to pick up his left hind leg and cross it over and in front of his right hind leg. His next step will be to uncross his right hind leg and step out to the right with it. The hind legs will continue crossing and uncrossing as long as you continue the cues. Meanwhile the left front leg stays in approximately the same spot and the right front leg walks a small circle around it. The turn on the forehand should also be practiced from the off side.

4.10

Sidepass In-Hand

The sidepass in-hand is a variation of the turn on the forehand. The difference is that you want the forehand to move sideways along with the hindquarters. The sidepass will give you the means to move your horse's entire body out to the rail when you are teaching longeing. And later in long lining, when you are teaching shoulder

in or half pass, you will use the outside long line to help you move your horse sideways. This will all come much easier if a horse has a fluid, relaxed association with sidepass in-hand.

In a sidepass to the right, let the horse's head and neck be slightly straighter, and although the head is still tipped slightly toward you, you will be exerting a bit of pressure to the right on the halter. Instead of cueing the horse on the ribs for the sideways movement, your cue will be more at the girth or shoulder area. The footfall pattern is two-beat with the left hind and right front reaching to the right at the same time. Next, the right hind and the left front will step widely to the right. Legs should always cross in front of their opposing leg and then uncross from behind. This is a valuable exercise for teaching the horse to move his entire body out of a space—handy when you are sending the horse out on the longe line the first time and don't want him to be on top of you!

Back

The back is a two-beat diagonal gait with the left front and the right hind moving together, and the right front and left hind working together. The horse should pick up his feet, flex his joints, and march crisply in reverse. He should not drag his toes, slide, or shuffle. His topline should stay rounded and low; he should not raise his head or hollow his back, as these are signs of resistance. The back is a maneuver that you must develop in the horse. He knows how to do it, but he doesn't have much reason to practice it on his own as he does the forward gaits. If you obtain a fluid yet crisp back in-hand, when it comes time to ask for one with the long lines, the horse will not have to learn several things at once. He will already know what a back "feels" like, and it will come easily to him in long lines.

To back a horse, stop him, turn around, and face his shoulder (Photo 4.11). Change the lead rope to your left hand and the whip to your right. Place the tips of the fingers of your right hand (or the butt end of the whip) on the point of his right shoulder and apply alternate pressure and release, and say "Baaaack." The fingertip pressure elicits a reflex action. Don't try to use halter pressure to teach a horse to back as this usually causes him to raise his head and hollow his back. After the horse has learned to back, using

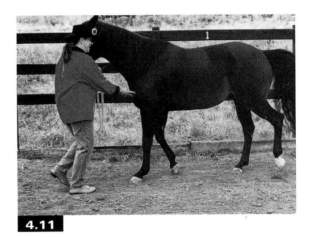

4.11

shoulder reflexes, you can use halter pressure as a "cue" to signal him to back.

Back a horse along the rail of your arena to help keep him straight. If his hindquarters start to swing off the straight line, straighten his body with the lead rope to make a slight adjustment of his head position. If his hindquarters start moving off to the right, move his head slightly to the right to align his body, and continue backing. Lead the young horse into an alleyway made of poles, railroad ties, or cones. Then back him out of it. This is a use of visual aids to show him what you want.

Sacking Out

Sacking out is a continuation of the lesson "Whoa." Once the horse has learned basic respect for restraint, you need to begin building his tolerance for stress. Stress is a demand for adaptation and is necessary for growth. You should gradually increase a horse's ability to withstand various stresses so that later, when he's confronted with them, he will be able to cope.

Because you use long ropes, 35-foot lines, saddle blankets, surcingles, saddles, and other items of tack on a horse, it's best to systematically introduce him to those objects and their movements and sounds. It only takes a few instances of a horse getting frightened of tack or tangled in ropes to undermine his confidence. A horse who has been well sacked out will have a much milder reaction when a surprise does appear, and there will be a much smaller chance of injury in the event of a muddle.

Self-preservation has taught the horse to be wary of unusual motions, sounds, sights, smells, and unfamiliar objects touching him. Setting up a specific group of lessons to help a horse overcome his natural fears will pay off in the long run. When working specifically on building confidence in the horse, never trigger active *resistance*. In other words, do not

stimulate him beyond his ability to cope. If you see the horse ready to blow up or flee, ease up and gradually work back up to his current tolerance level. Add more stress on another day.

Take the horse into a small training pen and show him a soft cloth jacket or a saddle blanket (Photo 4.12). Allow him to smell it. Then rub the blanket over his neck, back, and croup. Softly flap the blanket all over the horse on both sides (Photo 4.13). Stop and let the horse regroup if he seems ready to explode. Once the horse has accepted the soft, quiet item,

4.12

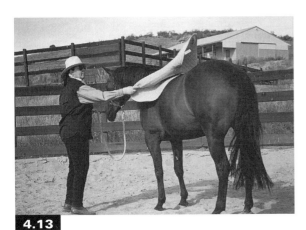

4.13

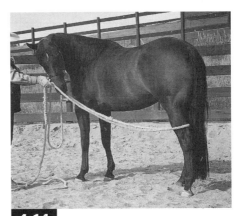

4.14

4.15

substitute a raincoat or slicker and begin the process again.

Still holding the horse in-hand, familiarize him with the presence of a rope all over his body. Throw the rope over his neck, shoulder, back, and hindquarters. Loop the rope around each of his legs and give a gentle tug (Photo 4.14). Let the rope slip down to the ground, especially around the pastern. Be ready to let one end of the rope go if the horse becomes afraid. Do this from both sides. Drag the rope on the ground so he can see and feel the rope from all angles. Loop the rope around each of his four legs. Let the rope move up and down each leg until the horse gets used to the sensation. Put the rope under the horse's tail, being careful not to

be in a dangerous position if he should kick. Let your horse learn that if he relaxes, the rope will fall away from his tail. The more you accustom your horse to ropes, the less chance you will have of a wreck during longeing or ground driving.

Show your horse that the whip is nothing to fear. While holding him in-hand, run the whip along his neck, back, and hindquarters. Also run the whip up and down the inside and outside of each leg (Photo 4.15). If you skip this step, the first time the horse sees a long longeing whip behind him, he may well panic. Once a whip has scared a horse, it is often more difficult to convince him that it is merely a training aid and nothing to fear.

Obstacle Work

Working a horse in-hand near and through obstacles builds confidence and familiarity between the two of you. Never ask a horse to negotiate an obstacle that is unsafe or unfair. Gradually build the horse's willingness to go forward through obstacles. Once the horse develops trust in you, there will seldom be refusals. Some of the most useful obstacle work specific to upcoming longeing and long lining includes teaching the horse to walk through mud puddles, over ground rails, over uneven terrain, next to a fence that has a jacket or tack hanging on it, and near other horses in pens and pastures.

Be prepared to go through the obstacle with the horse. If you plan to work on crossing water, wear rubber boots so you can show your horse that there is no reason to detour a water obstacle.

If you anticipate problems with a particular object, you may need to use a chain shank with the halter, and always carry a whip to help with forward impulsion. Use the whip to keep the horse up at your shoulder and the chain to prevent him from rearing or pushing forward. He will soon learn that the safest spot is next to you in proper position. If you make a horse understand the relationship between the driving and regulating forces during in-hand work, you ensure an easy transition to longeing and long lining.

Restraint

Restraint is limiting the action or movement of a horse by physical or psychological force. Your voice and hand can be an effective means of restraint, provided that the horse has been taught to respect and obey various commands and cues. Showing the horse that he must submit to certain restrictions is not meant to be harmful, but rather to protect the horse from his own natural instincts as he lives in the world of humans. Horses who have gone through well-planned sacking out and restraint lessons are more likely to remain calm when tangled in longe lines or a wire fence, have better manners for veterinary and farrier work, and tend to "test the limits" less often than those who haven't. Once a horse knows the meaning of the word "whoa" with the aid of restraint, he is much safer for himself and his handler in routine handling and management situations such as tying, hoof handling, grooming, and tacking.

Restraint begins the first time a foal is caught, and restraint lessons continue through halter training, tying, hoof handling, and include the introduction of a surcingle, cavesson, bridle, and side reins.

Tying

Tying should not be traumatic for either the horse or the handler. Whenever you tie a horse, there is potential for danger if he pulls, falls, or becomes trapped. That's why it is essential that you use safe tying practices. Although in most cases with horses who are accustomed to being tied you can use bull snaps or trigger snaps on the rope, consider using a panic snap (one with a sliding collar than can be released under pressure) if you are tying a horse who tends to be nervous when tied. Tie all horses with a quick-release knot, so that if you need to, you can instantly pull the end of the rope and release the horse. Keep a sharp pocketknife close at hand when you tie a horse so if all else fails, you can cut the rope if the horse is trapped. Practice using the knife beforehand on a thick, tight rope so you know how to wield it without injuring yourself or your horse. Wooden fence rails are usually not suitable for tying. A pulling horse could detach a rail and panic when it hits him or "chases" after him, injuring horse or handler.

Always tie a horse to a post or a well-constructed rail wither level or higher. This decreases the leverage a horse can obtain with his front legs and makes serious pulling difficult. If a horse is tied below the level of his withers and he wants to pull, he can get really good leverage with his front feet.

If a lead rope is tied too short, it causes the horse to hold his head and neck in an uncomfortable, cramped position. Tying too short could cause even a well-trained horse to panic and pull.

If the lead rope is tied too long, the horse can lower his head to the ground, move around too much, and possibly get his front leg over the rope.

To tie a horse in crossties across a barn aisle, stop him relatively straight with his head at the crossties. Turn and face the horse, with your left hand holding the lead rope. With your right hand, grab the near crosstie. Fasten the snap to the near cheek ring of the halter, not to the halter ring below the halter. Move the lead rope to your right hand. Step across in front of the horse to the off side, maintaining his position with the halter rope in your right hand, and reach for the far crosstie with your left hand. Fasten the snap to the far cheek ring of the halter. Remove the lead rope. Crosstie rings should be very stout, and the ropes attached to them should be fastened with a quick-release knot or a panic snap.

Positioning While Tied

When your horse is tied and you want to move him a few steps forward, step behind him, raise your hand behind his rump, and say "Walk up" or make a *click-click* noise with your tongue against your teeth. If he has had good in-hand lessons, he will move forward from this alone.

When he has taken a step forward, immediately lower your hand so he doesn't go too far. You might want to add the word "Whoa" if you think he will walk too far ahead.

To back a horse who is tied, use the same technique you did during in-hand work. Use your fingertips on the point of his shoulder while you say "Baaaack." Continue cueing as long as you want him to move back, taking care to note the restriction from the lead rope.

To move a horse over while he is tied, use the same technique you used for turn on the forehand during in-hand work. Slightly tip his head toward you and apply light intermittent pressure to his side. It is not uncommon for a horse to swish his tail, lock up, or even move into the handler the first time these aids are applied. Resist the temptation to use brute strength to move the horse over. If necessary, increase the intensity of your cue at the ribs. Be sure to work on both sides.

The better able you are to position your horse while he is tied, the easier it will be for you to position and control him while longeing and long lining.

5

TACK TACTICS

Although longeing utilizes some of the same equipment that you probably already have for in-hand work and riding, there are a few specialized items that are essential.

Longe Line

Your goal is to eventually work your horse in a circle 20 meters (66 feet) in diameter. That means the horse is working 33 feet away from you. That's why you need to use a 30- to 35-foot longe line (10 to 12 meters). The common 24-foot longe line might sound long until you realize that even when it is extended full out, the horse is only working on a 48-foot circle, which is too small for young horses or for cantering any horse. A 24-foot longe line is more appropriate for ponies.

My favorite longe line is 35 feet long and made from medium-weight, substantial cotton webbing. It has a swivel near the end that snaps to the horse's

5.1

5.2

5.3

halter, cavesson, or bridle (Photo 5.1). The swivel helps to keep the longe line from winding up into those tedious twists. The longe line has a large suede-covered handle for comfort and grip when I work my experienced horses out the full 35 feet. Remember, holding onto a longe line loop can be risky! When I work horses in smaller circles, I find the leather stops sewn every few feet along the line helpful for regaining control of a line that is being pulled through my hand by an over-exuberant horse (Photo 5.2).

A longe line with distance tags sewn into the line is useful for gauging distances and the size of the circle in which you are working the horse. Here the horse is being worked 20 feet away from the trainer; that would be a 40-foot-diameter circle (Photo 5.3).

Whip

Although most of the time a whip is used to just give a visual signal to a horse, occasionally it is used to produce an audible "pop" or "crack." And sometimes it is necessary to tap the horse with the whip.

To be most effective, a whip must be long enough to reach the horse. When a horse is working on a 66-foot-diameter circle, he is 33 feet away from you. The reality of a 35-foot whip is simply not practical in terms of function or weight. The choices boil down to three types of whips.

First is the standard one-piece whip; however, most of them are only about 10

to 12 feet long (5- to 6-foot shaft and 5- to 6-foot lash). The longest one-piece I've found is 14 feet (6-foot shaft and an 8-foot lash), which means you can reach a horse (adding a step forward and your arm length into the equation) who is working on about a 30-foot-diameter circle. For beginning work on a longe line, I suggest the longest, lightest one-piece whip you can find.

The second type is a two- or three-piece whip that you put together like a fishing rod. Although these are available in

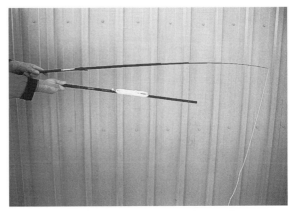

5.4 *Telescoping longeing whip. Whip on bottom is fully collapsed to its 3-foot storage and transport length. The lash is wound around lanyards. Only part of the 10-foot shaft of the top whip has been extended.*

lengths up to 15 feet, the ones I've used are so heavy and cumbersome that they are unacceptably fatiguing to the wrists and arms.

The third type of whip is a telescoping longeing whip that is made from hollow, nesting tubes of lightweight fiberglass-graphite (Photo 5.4). The whip retracts to 3 feet for easy carrying and transport and extends to a 10-foot shaft with a 17-foot lash, for a total of 27 feet in length. For free longeing and for advanced longeing on a full 20-meter circle, the telescoping whip is my favorite. (See the Resource Guide in the Appendix.)

Halter

What you put on your horse's head will determine how you communicate with him through the longe line. Although halters (*headcollars,* in Europe) are handy since every horse has one, they are not effective when it comes to training a horse to longe.

The main disadvantage of using a halter is that you really don't have control of the horse. It is very difficult to stop a horse with a halter when he is 30 feet away from you, unless he has already been trained to stop or wants to cooperate. If a halter is not perfectly fitted and adjusted snugly, it will shift on the horse's head and poke him in the eye whenever there is pressure on the longe line. That's why longeing with a halter is an option only for a very solid, well-trained horse, not a young, untrained horse.

You've probably seen it as often as I have—longeing with a halter and a chain. The main reason this is done, I am convinced, is economics. Most people already have a halter and a lead chain. It is not a sophisticated way to communicate with a horse on the end of a long line, however, because it is very difficult to set up a halter/chain combination that won't slip down a horse's nose or won't twist the halter if a horse tosses his head or pulls, or if the trainer has to give a tug.

But the biggest drawback is that most chain setups won't release and be inert when the horse is being obedient—the horse always has the pressure of the chain on his nose. There is no release or reward with this method because the contact and weight of the longe line exerts constant contact on the horse's nose with the chain. There just isn't a suitable application for halter/chain longeing, in my estimation.

Jaquima

A properly fitted and balanced jaquima delivers its pull from the heel knot area of the bosal and may be suitable for longeing the Western horse (Photo 5.5). A jaquima consists of a bosal, headstall, fiador, and a mecate, which is a combination of reins and a 12-foot lead. The bosal is the heavy

rawhide nosepiece of the entire jaquima, or hackamore rig. The bosal is suspended from a browband headstall that has had the throatlatch removed.

A knotted rope throatlatch, called the fiador, is substituted for the usual bridle throatlatch. There are three knots in the fiador: the hackamore knot, the fiador knot, and the sheet bend. The hackamore knot is tied in the fiador and it is affixed to the heel knot of the bosal. The fiador knot is tied and positioned 4 to 6 inches above the hackamore knot. The ends of the fiador pass through the headstall at the poll and are secured with a sheet-bend knot at the horse's near cheek.

A bosal can deliver an effective whoa signal. Care must be taken to ensure that the bosal is of the right size and diameter for the particular horse. Larger, thicker training bosals are suitable for young horses. The nose portion of the bosal should fit the contour of the horse's nose very closely. There should be two to three fingers' room between the rear portion of the bosal and the horse's jaw. This will allow the bosal to swivel back when the longe line is pulled, and relax and drop down when the longe line tension is slack.

5.5

Cavesson

A cavesson resembles a heavy, well-fitting halter and is the preferred headpiece for longeing English horses. "Breaking" cavessons are generally made of stout leather with heavy metal nosepieces and have straps to fasten them securely and keep them in position. This is important because during "breaking" it is often necessary to tug or pull quite hard on the line to control the horse. Lighter, simpler cavessons are also available for the very young horse, the already-trained horse, for use with a bit or bridle, and for use as a dropped noseband.

The traditional cavesson is made from leather, but nylon cavessons are also available. A longeing cavesson has a padded noseband with a jointed metal nosepiece that usually has three swivel-mounted rings attached to it. Generally the middle ring is used for longeing unless a horse carries his head extremely to the outside of the circle (Photo 5.6). In that case, the inside cavesson ring can be used to bend the horse inward on the longeing circle (Photo 5.7). The side rings are also used for side rein attachment or long line attachment.

Most cavessons have buckles for adjustment on both sidepieces. Unless a chin

5.6

pad is present, the noseband fastens with a single-thickness leather strap. The nosepiece is usually either plated steel, nickel-plated brass, or solid brass and is designed to control and guide the horse. Most are hinged in three places to allow the metal nosepiece to conform to a variety of nose shapes and sizes. The nosepiece acts on the nasal bone to control and guide the horse.

Besides having a nosepiece, sidepieces, and crown, there is nothing standard about longeing cavessons. A throatlatch

5.7

A face strap, which runs from the crown, browband, or sidepieces to the nose-piece, is designed to prevent the weight of a very heavy noseband from slipping down onto the horse's nostrils and to keep the noseband in position if a horse tries to pull away or bolt.

Bit straps are sometimes included for suspending a bit so the horse can carry it without requiring the use of a separate headstall under the cavesson (Photo 5.8).

strap, nice but not essential, keeps the cavesson positioned and secure and prevents the horse from pulling it off over his ears.

The essential cheek or jowl strap is like a second, lower throatlatch. Fastened snugly across the horse's cheek, this strap prevents the cavesson from twisting around and causing the sidepieces to bump into the horse's eye, which could easily occur when the longe line is pulled.

A browband, which I feel is essential, keeps the crown from sliding down the horse's neck.

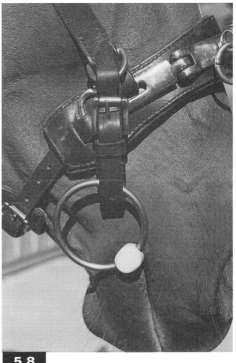

5.8

Fitting the Longeing Cavesson

For exercising a horse, the cavesson's noseband is generally positioned about midway between the prominent cheekbone and the corners of the horse's mouth. This is approximately two fingers' width below the prominent cheekbone and about three to four fingers' width above the nostrils. In this position, the noseband will be effective but won't interfere with the horse's breathing or risk damaging the fragile tip of the nasal bone.

When used in conjunction with a bridle and snaffle bit, the standard position of the cavesson is as previously described, above the bit.

Sometimes a cavesson is positioned below the snaffle bit like a dropped noseband. This is mainly for the control of a very strong horse but should be used by an experienced horse trainer and with discretion.

If a cavesson is used with a bridle, the noseband of the bridle is usually removed. The noseband of the cavesson goes under the cheekpieces of the bridle's headstall, but the crown of the cavesson goes over the crown of the bridle (Photo 5.9). If the noseband were buckled over the cheekpieces, it would interfere with the action

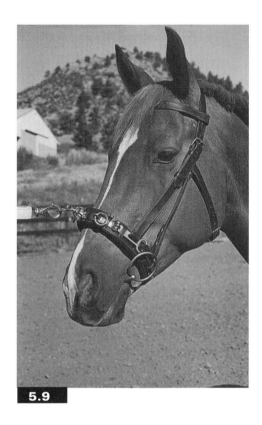

5.9

of side reins or long lines and could affect the comfort of the bit.

When using a double bridle, a light cavesson is in order; it should be located just above the headstall rings of the curb bit.

Protective Boots

Because of frequent missteps caused by physical inexperience, lack of coordination, and lack of conditioning, it is usually wise to protect the horse's front legs with boots. Splint boots with hard strike plates may prevent a fractured splint bone if the horse raps his inside cannon area with the opposite hoof.

Depending on their design, the boots might also protect the rear of the horse's leg, the flexor tendon area, from the blow of a hind toe if fractious behavior or uncontrollable galloping causes him to overreach.

Bell boots will protect the bulbs of the front heels from overreaching the hind hooves. Bell boots will also minimize trauma to the coronary band if the horse inadvertently steps on himself.

Sport boots are designed to support the flexor tendons during hyperextension, especially in deep footing at the canter or lope (Photo 5.10).

Before sport boots are applied, both the boots and the horse's legs must be very clean. Sport boots should be put on very snug to provide support and to keep debris from entering the boot. Because most sport boots are made of neoprene, which is heat-concentrating, they should be used for no more than about an hour at a time.

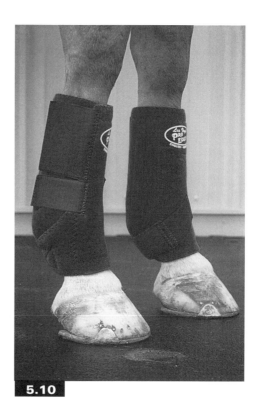

5.10

The Snaffle Bit

The word *snaffle* is derived from the Dutch *snavel* and the German *schnabel*, and means "to mouth" or "to break." The most common snaffle, the jointed O-ring, has four parts: two rings and a mouthpiece comprising two arms (Photo 5.11). Snaffles are mechanically simple bits that are appropriate for early basic lessons because they allow you to communicate with

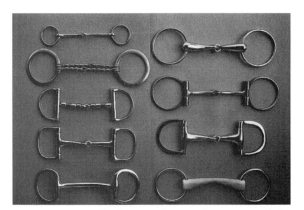

5.11 *Snaffle bits. Left row, from upper left: bradoon; double twisted-wire flat ring; copper and stainless roller D-ring; D-ring; mullen mouth eggbutt. Right row, from upper right: thick hollow-mouth wire ring; sweet iron with copper strip Don Dodge; thick hollow-mouth D-ring; contoured rubber bar ring.*

your horse in simple terms. A snaffle bit transmits pressure in a direct line from side reins or long lines (and later from your hands as a rider) to the rings and mouth-piece of the bit to the horse's mouth.

On a snaffle, there are no shanks (the vertical sidepieces on a curb bit to which the reins attach) that would create lever-age action. The snaffle bit operates via di-rect pressure only. The mouthpiece of a snaffle can be jointed or solid. The mis-conception that any bit with a jointed mouthpiece is a snaffle has given rise to

the misnomers: "long-shanked snaffle," "tom-thumb snaffle," and "cowboy snaffle". All of these are really jointed (or broken-mouth) curbs.

A snaffle is customarily used with a browband headstall that has a throatlatch and usually a noseband.

Snaffle Action

The snaffle is useful for teaching a horse to bend his neck and throatlatch so he can be turned in both directions. It is also use-ful for teaching a horse to flex vertically in the lower jaw, at the poll, and at the neck muscles just in front of the withers. Verti-cal flexion is necessary for gait and speed control as well as for stopping.

The horse's tongue is a large, thick muscle that is covered with soft, thin epithelial cells that make the tongue very sensitive and responsive to a bit. The snaffle acts mainly on the tongue and the corners of the mouth of an untrained horse.

The *hard palate,* or roof of the horse's mouth, is a mildly concave structure formed by 18 to 20 curved ridges with their convex edges pointing forward. If a snaf-fle mouthpiece is of a severe design, it could contact the hard palate, especially if the horse's mouth is restrained with a

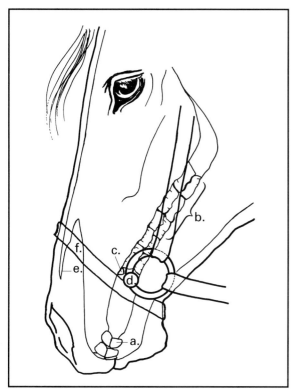

5.0 a. *Incisors* d. *Mouthpiece of bit*
　　　 b. *Molars* 　 *in front of premolars*
　　　 c. *Wolf tooth* e. *Nasal bone*
　　　　　　　　　　 f. *Noseband*

noseband. Some horses have a shallower palate than normal. The shallower or flatter the roof, the more sensitive the horse will be to certain types of snaffle bit mouthpieces.

The *bars* are the flesh-covered portions of the lower jawbone between the incisors and the molars. This is where the bit lies. It is the action of the snaffle bit on the bars of the horse's mouth that produces vertical flexion.

The nasal bone and cartilage and the chin groove are often affected when a noseband is used in conjunction with a snaffle. The horse who attempts to open his mouth to avoid bit action is thwarted by the pressure of the noseband (Drawing 5.0).

With two exceptions, the snaffle bridle does not usually pressure the poll. One exception is the gag snaffle. The reins and headstall of the gag are virtually one continuous piece. When the reins are pulled, the headstall essentially shortens. Pressure is exerted on the poll and corners of the lips. The gag is not appropriate for ground training.

The other exception occurs when the longe line is run through one bit ring, over the poll, and snapped to the other bit ring. When the longe line is pulled, there is upward pressure on the corners of the horse's mouth and on his poll. The longe line in this configuration acts like a gag snaffle and is not appropriate for routine training. Since it has severe effects, it should be used by experienced trainers for remedial purposes only.

With a regularly configured snaffle, when one line is pulled out to the side, let's say the right, the bit will slide slightly through the mouth to the right and the primary pressure will be exerted by the ring on the left side of the horse's face. This will cause him to bend laterally and turn right.

When the right line is pulled backward, pressure will be exerted on the right side of the horse's tongue, the right lower lip, the right corner of the mouth, the right side of the bars, and on the left side of the horse's face. This will tend to cause the horse to bend laterally and begin to flex vertically, so he shifts his weight rearward as he turns right.

When you pull backward on both lines, pressure will be applied to both corners of the mouth and across the entire tongue, and the bit may contact the bars and the lower lips. This causes a horse to flex vertically, shift his weight rearward, slow down, or stop.

Factors that Affect Bit Action

To assess the effect of a snaffle on a horse's mouth, it is helpful to know the factors that affect bit action and severity:

- The trainer's hands.
- The thickness of the mouthpiece.
- The weight of the mouthpiece.
- The texture of the mouthpiece.
- The shape or design of the mouthpiece.
- The type of metal.
- The width of the bit.
- The types of rings or cheeks.
- The adjustment of the bridle (and noseband, if used).

HANDS Your hands have the capacity to turn the mildest bit into an instrument of abuse or the most severe bit into a delicate tool of communication. Above all, good horsemanship is the key to a horse's acceptance of the bridle.

THICKNESS OF MOUTHPIECE In general, the thicker the mouthpiece, the gentler the action, because the pressure is distributed over a greater surface area (refer to Photo 5.11). A thin mouthpiece (1/16 inch in diameter) presses sharply into the nerves that lie just below the skin of the tongue and bars. A moderate mouthpiece (3/8 inch in diameter) is appropriate for most uses, is comfortable for the horse, and provides you with adequate control. A too-thick mouthpiece, like some hot-dog-sized rubber bits 3/4 inch or thicker, puts too much material in the horse's mouth and for some it's uncomfortable.

WEIGHT OF MOUTHPIECE Commonly, thick mouthpiece snaffles weigh more because of the additional material needed to make them. This can be an advantage because weight stabilizes the bit in a horse's mouth. Extreme weight, however, is unnecessary and can be tiring for the horse. Some large-mouthpiece bits are made hollow to provide mild action without excessive weight.

TEXTURE OF MOUTHPIECE Since the snaffle comes in contact primarily with the bars, the tongue, and the corners of the lips, the texture of the bit's surface will affect its severity. The surface of the mouthpiece can be smooth, wavy, ribbed, ridged, or rough (refer to Photo 5.11).

A smooth-mouthed bit makes even contact with the skin surfaces and underlying nerves. Such a bit slips around in a horse's mouth smoothly so there are no surprises and he can react fluidly without tension.

A twisted-wire bit's rough surfaces make interrupted and changing contact that can jangle nerves and rub tissues raw if used indiscriminately.

A mouthpiece with an uneven surface, as it moves from side to side, bumps the horse's mouth. This can serve to get his attention and control him or make him afraid. If a bit injures him, he may avoid contact with it by getting behind the bit.

Textured bits, such as a slow twist (one with a thick mouthpiece that has three or four twists to it), a scrub board (one with built-up stripes in the mouthpiece), a copper and stainless steel roller bit, a copper-wire-wrapped bit, or a twisted-wire snaffle may have their place in lightening up a tough-mouthed horse. But for standard training, a smooth mouth bit is most appropriate.

SHAPE AND DESIGN OF MOUTHPIECE
The shape and design of the mouthpiece can instantly affect a horse's response. Curved arms fit the contour of the horse's tongue better than straight arms or a straight-bar bit, but curved bits can make more contact with the sensitive bars (refer to Photo 5.11). Due to the variation in mouth structure, some horses need more

room for their tongues; a horse with a shallow palate needs less material in his mouth than a horse with a deeper palate.

A snaffle's mouthpiece can be solid or jointed. A solid straight bar generally doesn't allow adequate space for a horse's tongue. A solid mullen (gently curving) mouthpiece provides more tongue room and might give you more "whoa" power than a jointed bit but can cause a horse to become stiff in the jaw as he braces against the solid mouthpiece. A contoured rubber bit might be an option as long as it is not too thick (refer to Photo 5.11).

The movement of the arms, both at the joint and at the rings, encourages a horse to "mouth" the bit or "play" with it, that is, roll it and lift it with his tongue (but he is not supposed to bite it). This leads to a suppleness and relaxation of the jaw. That is why for suppling and lateral work, such as bending and turning, jointed mouthpieces are preferred over solid mouthpieces. A horse who actively works the bit with the tongue while keeping the mouth closed tends to have a moist, soft mouth.

TYPES OF METAL Since nerve impulses are tiny electrical transmissions, they are more efficient when sent through moist tissues. Therefore, a moist mouth is potentially a more responsive mouth. One thing that triggers the salivary reflex is the presence of food in the horse's mouth. When bridled, the mouthing of the bit, the construction of the bit, and the vertical position of the horse's head may also activate the glands. The more supple and vertically flexed a horse works, whether in a bosal, cavesson, halter, or bit, the more he will salivate (Photo 5.12)! This shoots the theory that it is the metal of the bit that causes a horse to salivate.

The metal of the bit, however, can either encourage or dry up the flow of saliva. Snaffles are commonly made of stainless steel, cold-rolled steel, and nickel or copper alloys. High-quality, bright stainless steel has a smooth surface that won't rust or pit and is very long wearing. Cold-rolled steel is a type of steel compressed to form a uniformly dense yet softer material than stainless. Cold-rolled steel is prone to rust; fans of this metal call the rust "seasoning" and say that the nutmeg-colored oxidation on the mouthpiece makes it sweet to the horse, thus the term "sweet iron." Silver show snaffles usually have cold-rolled steel mouthpieces but are called silver bits because of the

5.12

or incisors, or may encourage the horse to put his tongue over it. A bit that is too narrow can pinch the corners of the horse's mouth and put constant pressure on the bars and tongue.

The width of the bit is generally appropriate if, when the bit lies straight across the tongue (not peaked), there is 1/8 inch to 1/4 inch between the corner of the horse's lips and the junction of the rings and the mouthpiece on both sides of the bit.

TYPES OF RINGS OR CHEEKS   There are many options to consider when selecting snaffle sidepieces: O-ring, eggbutt, D-ring, and full cheeks. The O-ring, because of its loose action, is the most common type of snaffle used on young horses. The rings moving through the holes in the mouthpiece set up in the horse's mouth a "loose action" that keeps the horse mouthing the bit, attentive, and responsive.

Snaffle rings are usually made of flat stock or round wire. Round wire rings require much smaller holes in the mouthpiece than do flat rings. The large loose holes in a flat-ringed bit are notorious for pinching lip skin (Photo 5.13). And as flat rings move, they wear the edges of the

engraved silver that is inlaid on the rings. Copper alloys, with their reddish-gold hues, are used as solid mouthpieces and as strips inlaid in cold-rolled steel or stainless steel mouthpieces.

WIDTH OF BIT   The width of the bit can affect comfort and, inadvertently, the severity of the bit. A bit that is too wide for a horse may hang low and bang the canines

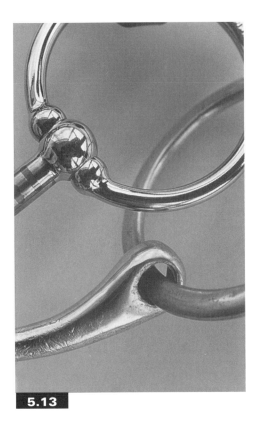

5.13

very large rings (those over 4 inches) sta-bilize the bit, they can put pressure on the wrong places of the horse's face—areas where there is virtually skin over bone. The smaller the rings (those under 1 1/2 inches), the greater the chance that the snaffle could be pulled laterally through the horse's mouth. Using a noseband, bit guards, or a "curb strap" can prevent this.

Most eggbutt or D-ring snaffles are constructed to avoid pinching skin in the corners of the mouth. The swivel mecha-nism is located in such a way that it does not contact lip skin.

A full-cheek snaffle comes with cheekpieces both above and below the mouthpiece of the bit (Photo 5.14). Cheekpieces should not be confused with shanks. The reins do not attach to cheek-pieces. A full-cheek snaffle delivers the most "lateral persuasion" of any bit. When the left line is pulled, the full cheek-pieces press on the right side of the horse's face and cause the horse to turn left. Full-cheek snaffles are designed to be used with keepers. Keepers are small leather tabs fitted to the bridle that hold the bit upright, presenting the widest and most curved surface of the mouthpiece of the bit to the horse's tongue. With the bit

holes in the mouthpiece to form rough burrs that can rub skin raw.

Some Western snaffles are constructed with a sleeve at the junction of the mouth-piece and the ring so that skin-pinching is minimized.

The rings of a snaffle put pressure on the sides of the horse's face and also help stabilize the bit in the horse's mouth. Three-inch rings are standard. Although

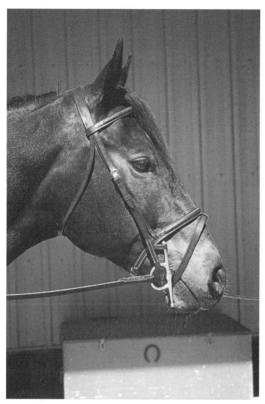

5.14 *Full-cheek snaffle with keepers and flash noseband.*

BIT WIDTH EFFECTS If the bit is too narrow for a horse, it can cause the ring-mouthpiece junction to press and rub against the corners of the lips. If a bit is extremely narrow, the mouthpiece is totally enveloped by the horse's lips, causing the rings of the bit to angle outward away from the sides of the horse's face.

With a too-narrow bit, the skin at the corners of the mouth often becomes raw or can be pinched by the mechanical action of the ring attachment. Also, if a bit is too narrow it can cause the rings of the bit to put pressure on the skin over the first premolars. All these factors can cause a horse to brace against the bit, toss his head, come above the bit, or resist in some other fashion. (Ask your veterinarian to put a "snaffle mouth" on your horse next time he floats his teeth. This involves rasping the front edge of the premolars so they are rounded, not sharp edged.)

When a bit is too wide and the bit is a jointed one, the joint in the mouthpiece can fold downward on the tongue if the bit is adjusted low and loose in the horse's mouth. This invites the horse to put his tongue over the bit, a difficult habit to break. If the bit is too wide and is adjusted high and tight in the horse's mouth, it can

upright, the mouthpiece hinges forward toward the incisors. When keepers are not used, the upper cheekpiece rotates forward, the bottom edge of the mouthpiece is presented to the horse's tongue, and the bit hinges downward toward the tongue. Full-cheek snaffles are most suitable for long lining.

HOW TO MEASURE FOR A BIT

The standard width for most English snaffles is 5 1/2 inches and for most Western bits, 5 inches. Bits are usually available in half-inch increments below and above this. To measure a bit, suspend it from a headstall so the rings are up, as they would be on the horse. Lay the mouthpiece flat on a table and using a tape measure, determine the inside dimension from one ring/mouthpiece junction to the other (Photo 5.15).

To measure a horse's mouth, use a piece of doubled baling twine, make a knot about a foot from one end and another knot 5 1/2 inches down the twine, leaving at least a foot on that end as well (refer to Photo 5.15). You can use this to get an estimation of the width of your horse's mouth. Simply slip the twine bit into your horse's mouth and see where the knots lie in relation to the corners of your horse's mouth. If your horse wears a 5 1/2-inch bit, there should be from 1/8 inch to 1/4 inch between the corners of his mouth and the knots on each side.

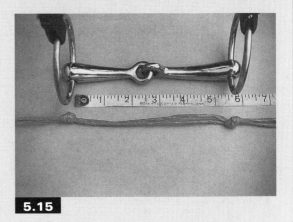

5.15

cause the horse to become obsessed with moving the joint of the bit backward with his tongue so he can bite the bit.

There is an advantage to having a bit *slightly* too wide for a horse's mouth. When a horse is turned by the pressure of one rein, the mouthpiece of the bit will slide through the horse's mouth, giving him a presignal before the ring or full cheek contacts the opposite side of his face. This keeps a light horse light and trains a young horse to react to the presignal, thereby preserving his mouth.

If a bit is very wide for a horse's mouth, however, the constant sliding back and forth disturbs the quietness of the communication with the horse's mouth and precludes finesse.

The Bridle

Often a cavesson (the lightweight bridle type) or dropped or flash noseband is used with a snaffle bit. In general, these items, in varying degrees, prevent the horse from avoiding the action of the bit by keeping the tongue under the bit, keeping the mouth closed, and stabilizing the bit's location. A noseband discourages beneficial mouthing of the bit. By keeping the mouth shut, however, it does prevent evaporation of saliva, thus preserving a moist mouth.

Proper adjustment depends on the style of the noseband, but care must be exercised not to exert undue pressure on the soft cartilage of the horse's nose. Most nosebands are designed to apply pressure to the nasal bone and the chin groove. More problems are introduced by a too-tight noseband than a too-loose noseband. Generally, you should be able to fit two fingers under the noseband. The horse won't be able to open his mouth, but he can work the bit and won't feel unduly restricted.

The cavesson or top portion of the flash noseband should be located about two fingers below the prominent cheekbone (Photo 5.16). The lower strap of the flash should be positioned below the bit and the buckle should be positioned at the bridge of the nose (Photo 5.17). If you position the buckle near the bit, it could cause rubbing; if you position it under the chin, the sweat and saliva will collect in the buckle and keeper and require more cleaning.

Western nosebands come in two varieties. One acts like a cavesson and the other like a dropped noseband.

5.16

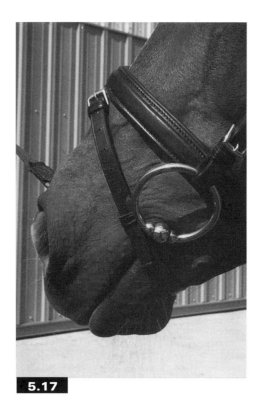

5.17

Adjusting the Bridle

The positioning of the snaffle should take into account a horse's tendencies, such as mouthing the bit, putting his tongue over the bit, chewing the bit, or biting the bit with his premolars. We're mainly concerned here with how high or low in the horse's mouth we locate the bit.

When the headstall is adjusted too short, the bit rides too high in the horse's mouth and is too tight against the corners of the lips and premolars. This type of fit is often characterized by a series of wrinkles at the corners of the horse's mouth. In fact, many trainers say they have a preferred number of wrinkles they like to see when fitting a bridle (Photo 5.18).

It's important to determine the horse's individual conformation, however, particularly the amount of space between the corner of the lips and the premolars. A short-lipped (shallow-mouthed) horse usually has enough room between the corners of his lips and his premolars to carry a few wrinkles in the corner of his mouth.

But with some long-lipped (deep-mouthed) horses, whose premolars are very close to the corners of the lips, using the two- to three-wrinkle rule might put the bit too close to the premolars. Skin can be trapped between the bit and the premolars and be painfully pinched.

In any case, when a bit is consistently adjusted tight, the tissues of the corners of the mouth may become thickened and hardened (i.e., "hardmouthed") and subsequently dull due to the constant pressure of the too-tight bit. Even if the pressure on the lines is released, there is no release of pressure on the horse's mouth! It's easy to understand why a horse so bridled doesn't

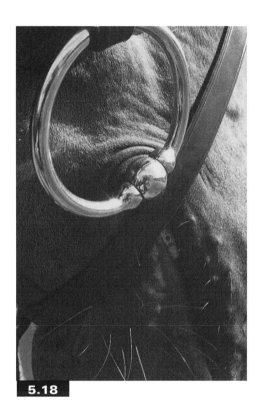
5.18

the mouth before it contacts the corners of the mouth. In a male horse, if the bit is extremely low, it could cause the bit to hit the canines. In any horse, a too-low bit is an open invitation for a horse to put his tongue over the bit.

With an intermediate to advanced horse, however, one who flexes at the poll and holds the bit in position with the suction created by his tongue on his palate, a bit positioned low in the mouth is not a problem. This is an asset because there the bit can act lightly on the tongue and bars rather than the corners of the lips. In fact, I prefer to allow some horses to learn to "carry" a bit as opposed to fixing a bit into position with a tight bridle adjustment.

When a bit fits just right, the mouthpiece (not the junction with the rings) makes a light contact with the skin at the corner of the mouth (Photo 5.19). The bit is positioned in the interdental space and the mouthpiece is of adequate width and thickness so the horse can comfortably carry the bit on his tongue.

If you see a horse try to put his tongue over a bit, do something quick! Don't let this habit form, as it is very difficult to break. Obviously, a tongue over

relax. What's the point, when there's no reward? The surface of the tongue may also become similarly desensi-tized when a bit is fit too tightly in a horse's mouth.

When the headstall is adjusted too long, it positions the bit too low in the horse's mouth. If the horse has not learned to pick up the bit with his tongue and carry it, the bit will just hang low. Signals to the bit could be disjointed and abrupt because the bit must first be lifted up in

5.19

5.20

the bit, rather than under, makes for poor communication with the snaffle. And a horse whose tongue lolls out the corner of his mouth while he is performing is very unsightly. Be sure the bit is the correct thickness and size, and the bridle is adjusted properly. Often the headstall needs to be shortened or a noseband added. In other cases, the horse may just require a bit that allows him more room for his tongue.

Young horses often exhibit odd behavior because they're not familiar with the bit. A young horse starts by carrying his head high and/or his nose extended out, and the bit touches only the corners of his lips. He will roll the bit, chew it, open his mouth and try to spit out the bit (Photo 5.20). This could indicate a need for dental work but is probably just a normal reaction. With more experience, he will likely accept the pressure of the snaffle on the bars and tongue. At that point, his head will lower with a slight convex curve to the topline of his neck and he will flex vertically at the poll.

Surcingle

A surcingle encircles a horse's heart girth, acting as a minisaddle and girth. For longeing, a surcingle provides a variety of places to fasten side reins. For ground driving in a horse's early training, the trainer runs long lines through the surcingle's side rings and then through the top terrets or rings as the horse advances.

Usually made of leather or cotton web, surcingles are available with a variety of features. Generally, surcingles have a top portion and a girth. The top portion is made up of the saddle and the sidepieces. The saddle consists of a padded pommel that sits on or behind the withers. The padding varies from a flat-profile (1/2 inch or less) saddle consisting of a thin layer of padding in the wither area to a high-profile (2 inches or more) saddle made up of two triangular-shaped blocks of padding. The padding and its covering vary from very soft to hard.

The saddle and sidepieces have attached to them various terrets, large D-rings, and small D-rings. The standard configuration is two large rings (or terrets) on top, two large rings on the sides, and three pairs of small rings in between. Terrets are rigid, fixed rings screwed into the top of the saddle at the approximate position a rider's hands would be (Photo 5.21). Terrets are very desirable for long lining because lines run smoothly through them. In lieu of terrets, most surcingles have large D-rings sewn, or sewn and riveted, into the top of the saddle (Photo 5.22). Some Ds are attached firmly enough to stand in an upright position—others are floppy. Like terrets, upright rings allow for free line flow.

5.21

5.22

In addition to the top terrets or rings, there is usually a set of large D-rings on the sidepieces of the surcingle for fastening side reins and for using long lines in lower positions. There are a varying number and size of smaller D-rings (customarily three pairs) on the top of the surcingle for attaching side reins and other training equipment.

Most surcingles have two standard billet straps on each side, such as are found on English saddles. Some surcingles have a single wider billet on each side. Most girths are a separate piece that can be replaced or substituted with a smaller or larger girth to fit various horses. The girth of a surcingle will vary in length (from 16 inches to 30 inches) depending on the design of the top portion of the surcingle

and the size of horse the surcingle is intended for. The standard girth has two buckles on each side to correspond to the two girth billets. Most girths have at least one D-ring sewn on the bottom side for the attachment of training equipment between the horse's front legs.

Surcingles can be used directly on the horse's back, with a surcingle pad, or with a regular saddle pad (Photos 5.23 and 5.24, respectively). Use the loops on the saddle pad to marry the surcingle and saddle blanket. If the blanket is not fastened to the surcingle, it can easily slip out from underneath and cause the horse to bolt or buck. A surcingle pad is a specially designed "channel-style" pad that locks into place under the surcingle.

Some surcingles are large enough to be used over the top of an English saddle (Photo 5.25). This might be a convenience if a horse needed to be long lined prior to riding and you didn't want to return to the barn to change tack, but this technique can result in problems. The surcingle has a tendency to slip from side to side when turning because the smooth leather covering of the surcingle padding offers no friction or grip against the smooth leather of the saddle seat. This

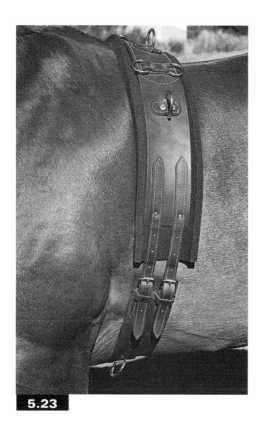

5.23

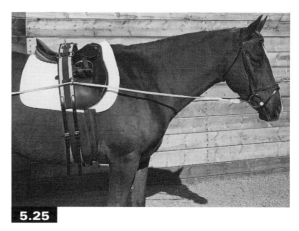

5.25

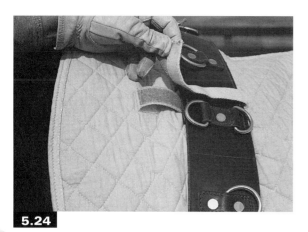

5.24

becomes a factor if a horse makes a sudden wrong move, as young horses do. You can avoid slippage by fastening the surcingle excessively tight, but then you've invited another problem—bucking! Also, when performing serpentines and flying changes, the long line of the "old bend" can get caught on the cantle of the saddle after the horse changes to the new bend. To remedy this, the trainer usually must stop the session and gather up the lines. Therefore, I greatly prefer using a surcingle by itself.

If you have access to an old driving harness, you can resurrect the saddle from the harness to use as a longeing and long lining surcingle (Photo 5.26). The saddle is often the last part of an old harness to show wear.

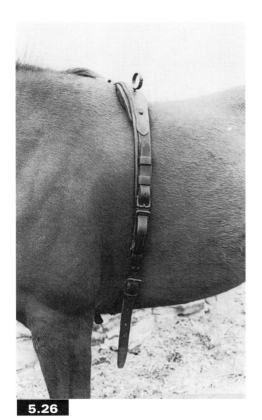

5.26

their use can lead to a dull mouth, leaning into or coming behind the bit.

The main materials in side reins are leather and cotton or nylon web. Elastic elements include rubber donuts, elastic inserts, rubber tubes, or rods (Photo 5.27). Leather is classic and looks, feels, and smells like horse tack. It's fairly easy to punch holes in leather side reins to increase their adjustability. Leather takes more care than web because sweat, dirt, and excessive dryness or wetness can weaken leather. There is a wide variation in the quality of leather. Poor-quality leather is more difficult to buckle and handle and often cracks, peels, or stretches when folded.

Side Reins

Side reins are adjustable reins that attach to the bit at one end and to the saddle or a surcingle at the other end. Adjusted and used correctly, they can be a valuable training aid used in conjunction with longeing. Many side reins have a stretchy section that offers some "give" to the horse's mouth. Solid side reins are for experienced horses and trainers; otherwise

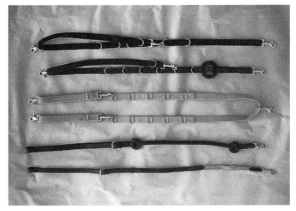

5.27 *Side reins. From top: quick-change web with no elastic; quick-change web with rubber donut; quick-change web sliding side reins; leather buckle with rubber rod; leather buckle with elastic inset.*

Web is low-maintenance and often stronger than leather. Nylon web is resistant to the damaging effects of dirt and moisture, does not stretch, and is very resistant to breaking. Cotton web, if abused, could theoretically deteriorate from the effects of dirt and moisture more readily than nylon, but I have had heavy cotton web side reins for years that are still in top shape.

It is not feasible to add holes to cotton webbing, and it is more difficult to add holes to nylon webbing than to leather. I've found the best way to add holes to nylon webbing is to heat an ice pick or nail and carefully melt a hole through the nylon web.

Elasticity. How much do you want side reins to "give"? When side reins are adjusted properly for light contact, the tension should approximate a rider's light feel on the reins. Using a spring scale, I have determined that when I'm riding and I have light contact on the bit, I exert about 6 pounds (combined pull, both hands) of pressure on the bit. When I exert strong contact, such as that needed to regain control, my combined hand pull measures 15 pounds. I have found that some donut side reins are too stiff to offer any give, and some rubber tube-style reins have so much

elasticity that they encourage a horse to play or misbehave. In general, I have found that elastic insert side reins approximate my 6-pound feel on the reins when I ride, so they are my recommendation for general purposes. If your side reins get a lot of use, you can have the elastics replaced after a few years.

Rubber donuts can range from very soft to rather stiff, but most are stiff. Some side reins with donuts have stops, a governor that stops the stretching at about a 3-inch increase in length. But it would take a real force to stretch the donuts 3 inches.

Rubber donuts tend to cause a lot of undesirable rein bounce if the donut is positioned near the bit. Simply turning the rein around and fastening the donut end to the saddle or surcingle eliminates donut bounce.

Side reins that have no elastic element are most appropriately used on experienced horses with educated mouths.

An exception to this are sliding side reins that, by virtue of their design and action, allow a horse to "give to himself" as he searches for a balanced way to carry his head and neck for each gait and extension or collection within each gait (Photo 5.28). Sliding side reins are

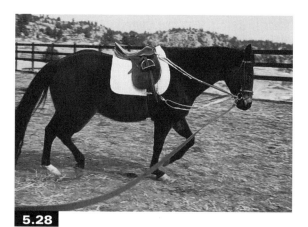

5.28

V-shaped, with the point of the V at the bit. The top leg of the V is usually at about the level of the breast collar D-rings. The bottom leg of the V is fastened at the girth. Each leg has evenly spaced D-rings and a snap for adjustment, so between the two legs, you usually have 12 or 14 adjustments.

The manner in which sliding side reins attach to the breast collar, bit, and girth varies according to the design. Some fasten by a snap. Others must be looped around a girth or through the bit ring and snapped to themselves. These are not as handy to use.

Sliding side reins are a great training aid. Most horses are not at all intimidated by them, and problems and accidents are virtually nil except for the possibility of a

horse stepping over the lower portion, especially if is positioned very low.

Side reins need to be constantly adjusted to accommodate variations in the size of horses and their levels of training. Also, within each work session, the reins will be changed depending on the phase of the work, the training style and discipline, and the gait. For example, I often go from long and low during the warm-up (approximately 42 to 43 inches) to a medium length for the working trot and canter (40 to 41 inches) to a shorter adjustment (38 to 40 inches) for the collected work, and then back to long for the cool-down.

Side reins adjust in one of two ways: with buckles and holes or with snaps and D-rings. Traditional side reins have buckles and holes. If there is space, more holes can usually be added to increase the range of adjustment of the reins. Usually there is more room to make them shorter. Buckle-style side reins usually are only offered in horse size.

A relatively new side rein design has a series of D-rings (usually six or seven) sewn on the rein and a snap that can be fastened to a D-ring for the desired length (like the sliding side reins described earlier). I like these reins because they are very quick and handy. I can stop my horse, make the adjustment, and be back on the longeing track in a matter of seconds. I like that I don't have to take off my gloves to use the quick-change-style reins as I do with most of the buckle-style reins.

When attached in a traditional manner (one end to the bit, one end to the saddle or surcingle), this style of side rein in horse size has about a 38- to 45-inch range, which is appropriate for most situations. For very collected work, however, or to use these side reins on smaller horses, the reins can be made as much as 10 inches shorter by attaching them in the following manner (Photo 5.29). Using elastic end reins as an example, take the attachment snap on the elastic end, run it through the bit ring, and snap it to the first D-ring near the elastic (the snap has been

transformed from an attachment snap to an adjustment snap!). If the snap on the other end of the rein is also attached to the same D-ring, you have in effect doubled the reins and shortened them by 10 inches. Of course, you also have all of the adjustments in between.

Miscellaneous Tack

Girth Loops for Side Reins

If you are attaching side reins to an English saddle, you usually have two choices. One is the breast collar D-ring that is located near the pommel. Although that position approximates the level of the rider's hands, often what is needed during training is a lower position to discourage the horse from hollowing his neck and coming above the bit and to encourage the horse to lengthen and stretch down. That's why the most popular place to attach side reins to an English saddle is through the billets or around the girth just above the saddle pad strap.

With side reins that have snaps on both ends, it's quicker and easier to attach them by using girth loops, which are leather or web loops that have a sewn-on metal ring (see Chapter 6, Photo 6.51). Even when using traditional buckle side reins, girth

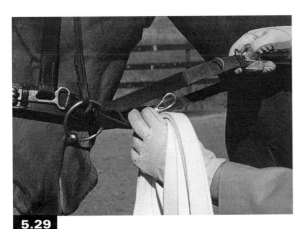

5.29

loops are much easier to use than feeding the side rein strap under an already-tightened girth.

Girth loops also act as side rein extenders. For example, if you own a pair of standard-length side reins and own an Arabian and a warmblood, you might be able to use the standard reins on the warmblood if you use girth loops that can increase the resulting length by as much as 10 inches.

Stirrup Keepers

Stirrup keepers are an alternative method of keeping the stirrups on an English saddle from bouncing and sliding down the leathers while longeing. Traditionally, the stirrups are tied in place with the stirrup leathers. A stirrup keeper strap is about 15 inches long with a snap on each end. The snaps fasten to the stirrup irons and run over the top of the saddle.

Bucking Strap

The stirrup keeper strap can also be used to form a handhold at the front of an English saddle. Snap one end of the strap to one breast collar D and the other end to the other D. Let the strap rest at the front of the saddle until it's needed, such as during a longe lesson.

Curb Strap-style Longe Straps

Attached via snaps or buckles to both rings on the underside of a snaffle bit, the straps have a D-ring or swivel ring at the center of the strap to attach the longe line (see Chapter 6, Photo 6.44). They are usually made of web or leather. The attachment of the longe line doesn't have to be changed on a curb longe strap when you change direction. However, there is greater pressure on the outside ring of the snaffle if a horse pulls, which causes him to face away from you rather than toward you. Also, the bit tends to collapse with a strong pull, peaking upward in the horse's mouth and pressing strongly on the bars. Therefore, this style strap is best for routine longeing of a trained horse who doesn't pull or lean.

Buckle-style Longe Strap

This style strap buckles to the bit and cavesson and has a D-ring to attach the longe line (see Chapter 6, Photo 6.43). The result is less direct pulling on the bit, yet a stable feel of the contact with the horse. It protects the bit from metal-to metal jangle and wear. Although the longe line must be changed to the other side when changing direction, the effect of the strap is the best option when you want to longe with a bridle.

6

THE LONGEING
PROGRESSION

The art of longeing should be approached with as much consideration and importance as riding itself. To longe well, you must constantly observe a variety of details about your horse's behavior. You then need to respond appropriately with aids that support and guide the horse, all the time reevaluating and revising as necessary while the horse is in motion. Each horse learns at a different rate, has inherent talents and weaknesses, and requires an individually tailored plan. You will need to design a plan for each horse.

Even though each horse requires a slightly different approach and a custom training plan, it helps to have a master ground-training plan, from basic to more advanced work, to serve as your guide. This chapter and the next provide the master framework that you can tailor to your needs. (For a progression of specific exercises, refer to *101 Longeing and Long Lining Exercises: English and Western.*)

If you are training a dressage prospect you might need to bypass free longeing for lack of a round pen but you might incorporate a very thorough side-rein program that spans 2 years or more. If you are developing a western pleasure horse, you might hold a lot of sessions in the round pen and skip the use of side reins and long lining. The beauty of having and understanding a complete program is that you can modify and adapt according to your needs.

If you have a horse four years of age or older, you can start at square one and work at the pace dictated by your experience and your horse's responses. If you have a horse two years of age or older, you can begin right now and work through the various stages until you get to the phase that uses side reins. Save that stage for the horse's four-year-old year.

Can a yearling be longed? Generally, during the fall of the yearling year, when a horse is about 18 months old, light longeing can be used mainly to develop obedience, responsiveness to your body language, and a familiarity between you and the horse. It shouldn't be thought of as a means of conditioning a horse, building muscle bulk, or tiring him out so you can handle him. This would be too much stress for a young horse.

Before you longe any horse younger than 24 months of age, examine his knees and fetlock joints. Some young horses have "open" knees; that is, the growth plates of the bones are still actively adding on bone. With such a horse and with any horse who otherwise seems to be a slow developer, I'd suggest postponing longeing until the spring or summer of the two-year-old year. Pasture turnout would be a better exercise option until then.

The Overall Plan for the Young Horse

When any horse is started, it will take approximately one month to teach him very thoroughly the basics of longeing.

With horses under two years of age, the sessions can be held two to three times a week but should be only 5 to 15 minutes long and contain no loping or cantering. I prefer to conduct the first group of longe lessons free in a 66-foot–diameter round pen. If a round pen is not available, the work will need to begin with a longe line.

Start the horse on a 10-foot line and work concentric circles for five-minute sessions for a week or so. As soon as the horse is ready, let the line out to 20 to 30 feet while still maintaining control. After a few weeks, increase the longeing time to 15 minutes per session and be sure that if you are using a longe line, it is at its full 30- to 35-foot length.

In the early lessons, emphasize good habits and quality of interaction instead of quantity of time going round in circles. Take your time grooming and tacking up the horse. Work on good manners when the horse is being haltered, when he is tied or crosstied, when boots are being put on, in-hand manners when being led to the longe area, and so on. During the actual longeing, mainly work on obedience at the trot, walk, and halt.

With two- and three-year olds, the sessions can be increased in frequency or time but not both. Loping and cantering for short periods should be introduced.

When a horse is developed enough to add cantering, do it gradually. You will want to increase the length of the sessions to about 20 minutes. First, warm up the horse thoroughly at the trot. The canter departs should be from a trot at first. Limit the canter work to about two circles at a time, two times in each direction.

Older horses, especially once they are conditioned to longeing, can be longed five or six times a week if the sessions are kept around 15 minutes. If the horse requires longer longe lessons of 25 to 30 minutes, for example, it would be best to limit the frequency to two or three times a week.

When the horse has learned the basic gaits, transitions, and has good manners, you can work specifically on refining various longeing maneuvers.

Longeing Methods

There are various methods of longeing, each with its advantages and disadvantages and each requiring slightly different equipment.

Free longeing must take place in a round pen because the loose horse is worked around you in a circle, but without a longe line. The pen itself creates the circle, and since you have no longe line to signal the horse, you will use body language and whip positions to communicate with him. Free longeing is an excellent way to establish your relationship with a horse in simple terms.

Longeing with a halter and longe line is a rather unsophisticated way to casually longe a well-trained horse, but it is not a very effective way to train a horse to longe. You have very little control when you use a halter and you will not be able to influence a horse's form while he is working. This method does, however, require the least amount of specialized equipment and can theoretically be performed anywhere that you can control the horse. But if you have to stop a horse who doesn't want to stop, you might find the amount of jerking or pulling required is hard on you and very ineffective.

Longeing with a bosal is a viable option. If the jaquima and bosal are well fitted, they will be a great improvement over a halter and might be more suitable than a cavesson for certain horses.

Longeing with a cavesson is the most traditional English method of longeing. It provides you with more control via the close-fitting weighted nosepiece of the cavesson. Once a horse has learned the basics, you can introduce a surcingle and then attach side reins from the cavesson to the surcingle to accustom the horse to pressure before putting a bit in his mouth. You can introduce a bridle and allow the horse to carry it while you control him with the cavesson.

Longeing from a bridle is different than longeing *with* a bridle. If you attach the longe line to a bridle and that is your means of controlling and communicating with the horse, that is longeing *from* a bridle. It is an unstable and potentially severe method of attachment and should be reserved for experienced horses and trainers. Should an inexperienced horse misbehave while being longed from a bridle he could injure his mouth if he pulled, bolted, fell, or had to be sharply reprimanded for his behavior. Longeing *with* a bridle is a more suitable arrangement. This is longeing the horse from the cavesson while he is wearing a bridle. Side reins can be attached to either the bit or the cavesson, but the point of longe-line attachment is the cavesson.

Training or exercising? The techniques used for *training* a horse on the longe line and *exercising a trained* horse on the longe line are often very different. Almost any training session will go better if a horse is first turned out to burn off surplus energy. The untrained horse should go through a thorough, progressive developmental training program on the longe line. Care always

FREE LONGEING GOALS

Move forward.

Stop.

Turn (Natural tendency will first be away from trainer).

Transitions and all gaits appropriate for level of horse's training.

Turn toward trainer.

(See *101 Longeing and Long Lining Exercises* for specific free longeing exercises and instructions.)

should be taken when selecting, fitting, and adjusting tack.

With a trained horse, you might be able to conduct a trouble-free and productive longeing session by using only a halter and a longe line, but as mentioned earlier, this would not be a good choice for a young horse. Just because you can snap a longe line to the inside halter ring of a trained horse and have a crackerjack session, don't think that a young horse will understand or benefit from such an approach.

Free Longeing

Free longeing requires minimal tack but maximum facilities. Although the only tack you really need is a longeing whip, because the horse is working without a longe line, you will need a circular pen at least 50 feet in diameter. A 66-foot pen is ideal as it is the equivalent of a 20-meter circle. Because there is no tacking up, prep time for free longeing is short.

It is the least complicated form of longeing, with less chance for conflicts from tack. It is easier on the trainer because there is no longe line to hold, keep organized, or tug. Free longeing helps with catching lessons and with teaching a horse to face you. These valuable lessons carry over to when a horse is free in a pasture.

One drawback of free longeing is that you don't really have control of the form of a horse's movement. Although a perfectly conformed horse who is active might move in pretty good form naturally, most horses have imbalances and stiffness that cause them to travel counterflexed, hollow, fast, or crooked. Most horses benefit from training aids that help develop good form. Also, with free longeing, since the horse is "free," if he did get out of the pen he would be loose. That is why a round pen must be strong and at least 6 feet tall, so that a horse does not even try to get out of it.

When free longeing, many horse owners are tempted to teach their horse to come to the center of the pen. I not only strongly discourage you from teaching this lesson but I also encourage you to always keep the horse on the longe circle pointed in the direction he is headed unless you are asking him to turn. It takes only a few lessons of coming to the center to quit work or get a treat to teach a horse that the center is a pretty good place to be. Some horses will then always be looking for a reason to quit and head to the center, much like a gate-sour horse who wants to stop by the arena gate and leave!

First Free Longe Lesson— Twelve-Month-Old Quarter Horse Gelding

Before beginning the first free longeing lesson, turn the horse out for exercise, then review a few in-hand maneuvers, and end with a bit of head handling. I never leave a halter on a horse in a stall, pen, or pasture, but I prefer to leave the halter on the horse for free longeing, provided that the halter is well-fitted and there is no place for the horse to get the halter caught in the training pen. The halter makes a formal association with the horse that "training" is taking place. It also gets the young horse used to wearing something on his head that he should not try to rub off, even if he gets sweaty.

Even though this yearling was turned out previously for exercise, he is still full of beans. I take him into the round pen, leave him on the rail and return to the center of the pen. When I step toward him to move him off, he shows his stuff (Photo 6.1). When I ask him to quit goofing around, by stepping in front of him, he does what most horses do until they are taught differently—he turns away from me (Photo 6.2). This is a typical young horse behavior. He doesn't "understand" anything yet and is just acting from instinct—a bit of uncertainty and he assumes the predator-avoidance posture, which is to turn away and put his best defense (hindquarters) between him and his source of uncertainty. Although any time a horse turns his hindquarters toward you it is potentially dangerous, I don't make a big deal of it here until he has had a chance to figure things out.

6.1

6.2

6.3

After he burns off some more energy, I step back so as not to turn him, and ask him to stop. He shows that he is aware of my presence at the center of the pen (Photo 6.3). I put a lot of emphasis on stopping and standing because it relaxes a horse and helps him to develop patience.

Paying attention and being aware of the trainer in the center of the pen is the first goal of free longeing.

I prefer to work a horse first in both directions at an active trot. The walk does not have enough impulsion to keep things focused and forward and the lope is usually too exciting and unbalanced for a young horse to handle. At the trot, I let him find his balance and carriage naturally.

At first, like most untrained horses of any age, he travels with a high head, face line about 50 degrees in front of the vertical, back hollow, and croup high and way behind the movement (Photo 6.4). This results in very short, choppy strides. Ouch,

6.4

6.5

6.6

painful to watch! Some horses might stay at this stage through several lessons because of their conformation or natural tenseness.

By remaining relatively inactive in the center of the pen, however, I let him find the various body-carriage options on his own. Soon, by being allowed but not pushed to find another way of moving, he progresses to an energetic, reaching trot (Photo 6.5). Although his head is still high, he is reaching under more with his hind legs, which starts to take the hollowness out of his back. This is a much more productive way of moving and easier for me to watch!

Left to his own devices, the yearling slows his trot even more, lowering his entire frame and rounding his topline even further (Photo 6.6). He has lowered his head considerably, although his poll is still the highest point of his neck, which is desirable. His face line is now about 20 degrees in front of the vertical, which is ideal for a free-moving horse. He has shortened his stride somewhat and has produced the easiest trot to ride of the three he has shown. This would be a very good trot for this yearling Quarter Horse gelding to work in, as it would develop his musculature and topline in a productive fashion.

And now a bonus and a sign that the session was productive. After less than 15 minutes of longeing during his first free longe lesson, this yearling is trotting with his nose almost lowered to the ground (Photo 6.7). The manure that he deposited during his very first turn early in this sequence might be what is interesting him, but the fact that he is relaxed enough to trot with his head that low shows that he worked naturally through all the stages of carriage. He is finishing up by giving his back and topline muscles a good stretch.

Be ecstatic if your young horse's first session goes like this. He did not become exhausted and sweaty, yet he learned some of the first keys to longeing.

Fourth Free Longe Lesson— Two-Year-Old Quarter Horse Gelding

This gelding, a full brother to the yearling in the previous sequence, is a much "hotter" horse when it comes to moving. If the yearling is a pleasure horse, this one is a racehorse. This is his fourth free longe lesson and they all started out the same. When I turn him loose, he calmly moseys over to the rail and begins walking. But some internal or external stimulus, which to a human observer seems to be 99 percent imagined, startles him after about 60 seconds and he takes off at a full gallop as though he really has somewhere to go (Photo 6.8). With this horse, I do not take a whip into the round pen; I use arm signals only.

6.7

6.8

(*Historical Note:* Before lesson number three, I turned the gelding out in the round pen and left him on his own. I wanted to see what he would do without a human in the pen. He went full bore for almost 30 minutes, mainly to the left. Since racing just gets a horse tired and sweaty and tends to perpetuate an orbit of accelerating, unbalanced movement, it is not productive work. When you find you have a racer on your hands, the best thing you can do, provided you are working in a very safe, strong pen, is to turn the horse several times into the rail.)

This horse watches my every movement. When I am over 30 feet away from him, I just lift up my left arm and wiggle my fingers; he slams on the brakes (Photo 6.9). After two high-speed turns, his next turn is much calmer. Of course, he is still turning toward the rail, which I am not specifically requesting. However, my goal is first to get him to feel confident traveling slower, smoother, and in balance. Later, I will work on both inside and outside turns.

After the three turns, I stop him with just an extended arm and the voice command, "Whoa" (Photo 6.10). He turns his head to face me, which is ideal. I want his attention to be on me, but I want his body to stay on the track of the circle, not to step toward me.

I lower my arm and we stand looking at each other, neither of us moving (Photo 6.11). This is a good sign. I verbally praise

6.9

6.10

him with "Good boy." Notice that this horse, although a very spirited, "hot" horse, does not have to be exhausted to learn. This is only three minutes into the session.

After the turns and stop, the horse is ready to settle down for some productive work. Here is a calm but energetic trot that will be productive (Photo 6-12).

6.11

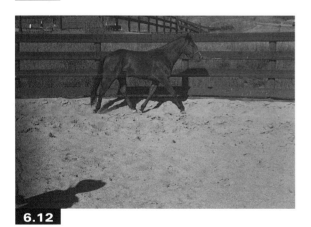

6.12

Experienced Five-Year-Old Quarter Horse Gelding

Eventually the free longeing work should begin and proceed calmy and deliberately. Here's how to turn a horse to the inside. The gelding was tracking to the right at a trot. To stop him, lower the whip (which is in your left hand) and bring it behind you at the same time you say "Whoa" (Photo 6.13). If necessary, you can add a raised right arm to help you stop the horse. When the horse comes to a complete stop, let him settle for a second before you ask him to turn.

Change the whip behind your back to your right hand and step to the front of the horse as you say "Turn," using a very circular voice. The raised whip and singing voice command encourage forward movement (Photo 6.14).

6.13

6.14

6.15

6.16

6.17

Maintain your position without being too aggressive and you will "peel" the horse off the rail (Photo 6.15). As long as the horse is turning to the inside, he is doing what you want, so give no further cues because you could confuse the horse.

When the horse is facing you, you can begin lowering your whip and moving forward and in the new direction (Photo 6.16). Be careful not to give an accidental cue with your left hand that could turn the horse.

As you ask your horse to walk, lower your whip and go back to your position at the center of the round pen (Photo 6.17).

Within a few strides ask for a lope from a walk by raising your whip and using your voice command (Photo 6.18). Mine is "Let's go." (The photographer's vantage point makes it look as though I am ahead of the gelding's motion, but I am even with his hip to drive him forward.) This horse strikes off with his hind legs well under his body and with an elevated forehand but not a high head.

A horse's natural tendency is to either rush into the transition and race fast out of balance or to throw his head up (coming above the bit if he's wearing a bridle), hollow his back, and canter in short, springy strides with no reach or drive. You want some of the first "called for" canter transitions to be balanced. To make a positive association with that transition, develop good habits. Don't scare or rush the horse into a lope and don't use the lope or canter in an improper form as a means to tire the horse.

To trot, lower the whip and use the command "Ta-rot" (Photo 6.19). Note that I've made sure my left hand is out of sight. If you find that your arm waves out while you are walking or using the whip with your other hand, you might be inadvertently giving your horse a cue to turn. This is one way to "remind" your arm to stay at your side. Each horse is different in his whip response. This alert, responsive gelding does best when I lower the whip all the way to the ground for the transition and then bring it back up to horizontal to maintain an energized trot. Again, I want to remind you that the perspective makes it seem as though I am ahead of the horse's movement, but in fact, I am at his hip.

6.18

6.19

The Longe Line

A longe line will give you added control over your horse, but it is one more thing you have to keep track of. When you add a line, you have the means to definitively teach your horse not to turn his butt toward you when you ask him to turn. You will be able to prevent the horse from ducking to the outside and turning into the rail. You can also begin to correct counterbend and add inside bend. The concept of inside bend can be a simple series of takes and gives to get the horse turning slightly into the circle. But perhaps most important, provided your horse is trained, a longe line will allow you to longe him in an open area such as an arena or pasture.

A longe line presents several safety hazards. Your horse could become tangled in the line or simply get one leg over the line, which could result in a frightening experience and/or a rope burn. That's why sacking the horse out to rope is essential because it will minimize any reaction to restriction by ropes. The line could also tangle your own feet or arms and, coupled with a frantic horse, could turn into quite a wreck.

Before You Add the Longe Line

Before you attempt to longe your horse with a longe line and a halter or cavesson, teach him how to bend to the left and right on a long rope. This will get him used to a long rope controlling him and will give you an indication of how he might react on the end of a longe line.

You will perform this exercise on the near side first, but my photo sequence demonstrates the exercise on the off side.

Standing on the off side, snap a 15- to 20-foot rope to the throat ring of the horse's halter. You can attach the line to one of the cheek rings if you feel your horse will require more of a lateral cue, but then you will have to change the point of attachment each time you change direction. I prefer to use the throat ring, and most horses learn the lesson well with the rope attached there.

Tell your horse "Whoa" and then step to his hindquarters and give a soft tug on the rope, which should cause him to turn and face you.

Do this on both sides.

Then stand on the off side of the horse and place the rope over his neck so the rope is on the near side of his body (Photo 6.20).

Tell your horse "Whoa," step to his hindquarters, and draw the rope along his topline and croup (Photo 6.21). Take care you don't pull the rope or you could cause the horse to move. Make sure there is plenty of slack.

If necessary, repeat "Whoa" as you step at least 10 feet from your horse's off side. Lightly tug on the rope, which should cause your horse to turn to the left (Photo 6.22).

Gather up the rope as the horse quietly turns to the left (Photo 6.23). Let the horse find the answer slowly the first time.

Continue gathering up the rope until the horse has turned around and is facing directly away from you (Photo 6.24). Be aware that you are in a potentially dangerous zone. This is a first session that demonstrates the stiffness with which the horse turns. The goal is to have the horse arc the body from head to tail and drop her head.

Continue exerting a bit of pressure on the rope until the horse faces you and the exercise is complete (Photo 6.25). She comes around without any fuss, but her body has been stiff through the whole exercise. At this point I would walk up to her rather than ask her to walk up to me.

6.20

6.21

6.22

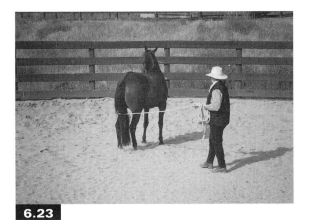

6.23

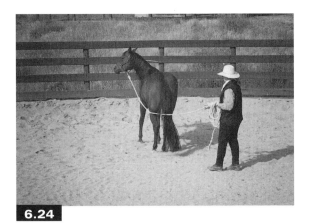

6.24

6.25

Now step to the near side and perform the exact same exercise. Continue to alternate sides until the horse bends equally well in both directions without resistance. Every horse will initially be smoother in one direction and stiffer in the other. Many horses will hold their heads up and their bodies stiff in one direction. This will alert you to tendencies and potential problems in the upcoming work.

After completing this exercise, your horse will be better prepared for the sensations that she will likely encounter in longeing, and will tend to respond with cooperation rather than resistance.

You should also review sacking out with ropes to prevent the spaghetti twirl: work from the off side and make a strong connection between the in-hand voice commands "Walk on," "Whoa," and "Easy."

Longeing Configuration

When longeing with a line, the configuration that the trainer and horse make is like a piece of pie rotating around a pie pan (Photo 6.26). The round pen is the pie pan. The horse is the crust, the trainer the point of the slice of pie, the longe line is one side of the piece, and the extended whip is the other side. The hand holding the longe line

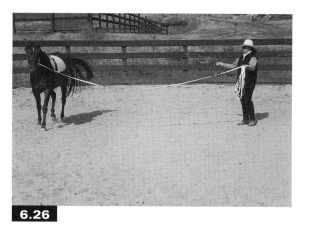

6.26

6.28

6.27

guides the horse, regulates impulsion, and helps to balance and shape the horse. The hand holding the whip provides impulsion

(Photo 6.27). The trainer's position in relationship to the horse is at or behind the midpoint of the horse's body, catching the horse between the driving aid (whip) and restraining aid (the longe line).

Although the end goal is to have the horse work around you in a circle, at first, in all stages of longe line training, you might have to work concentric circles with your horse. That is, you will walk along side your horse with the longe line out about 10 feet (Photo 6.28). This gives the horse the idea that you want forward motion. Gradually you will let out more line, and you will step closer to the center of the round pen so the horse is traveling more on his own (Photo 6.29). Eventually you will be able to stand in the center and have the horse work around you

(Photo 6.30). Just because you have used this technique on one phase of longe line training doesn't mean you shouldn't have to repeat it each time you introduce something new. It's a reassuring review for the horse.

6.29

6.30

Prevent Anticipation

To prevent anticipation, take your time when you first start a horse on the longe line. Be sure to have the horse stand patiently for a time while you fiddle with the line and whip. Whistle, sing, recite your breaking patter, and fiddle around with your tack. I like to methodically loop my longe line, then drop it on the ground and start all over again.

Let the line out to "bait" the horse with the opportunity to take off, but be prepared to catch him. If he moves, bring him back to the same starting point. Review your 'Whoa" on the long line lesson. Be careful that you are not giving him accidental cues with your whip. When you feel the horse has accepted the lesson that he must stand still until you ask him to move off, start making your moves less cautious because some day you'll drop a whip or the line, and you don't want that to set your horse off. If a horse continues to move his hindquarters away from you and face you when you try to begin, instead of starting out in the center of the pen, take him to a rail to help you hold him straight until you start him. Later you can start the lessons in the center.

Walk

When you first start training a horse to longe, start with the horse along the fence of your pen so he goes forward and not sideways. You might have to stand a little rearward to encourage impulsion and not confuse the horse. If you stand too far toward the horse's head, he might read this as body language to stop or turn. With the arm holding the longe line extended, inviting forward movement, and the whip extended toward the hindquarters, use your voice command "Walk on." Walk along with the horse, then in concentric circles, and finally have the horse work around you in a circle. Save the concentric circle technique for times when you need to increase the horse's impulsion or when you want to use it to teach the horse to extend or move out in a particular gait. If you constantly stay after a horse, your signals will lose their effectiveness.

Trot

Although it seems as though walking would be the first thing you teach your horse, sometimes it is not. If your horse were very calm and well mannered, asking him to walk in each direction with

a couple of halts here and there would be a great first longeing lesson of about five minutes.

Because of the lack of impulsion at the walk, however, many horses tend to turn or stop, which you want to avoid. So, if you think your horse can stay calm, begin the trot after a few steps of walk. This will result in fewer stalls outs and unwanted turns, and less confusion. Your horse will learn to keep going forward with continuous motion.

If your horse is trotting and you want him to walk or stop, use the body language you used in free longeing.

Turning to the Inside

When you add a longe line, you have immediately gained a positive means to control which way a horse turns when you call for a reverse. If you didn't make this distinction in free longeing, you can make it here.

Always make the first turns from a halt. Have the horse stop, wait, and relax while you switch the whip behind your back. Be sure you maintain some tension inward on the line. Give the voice command "Turn" using circular sounds, step to the horse's forehand, and present the whip as a cue to turn. With some horses, the first turn comes easier on a 30-foot line than it would on a 10-foot line, as many horses feel crowded and stiffen when facing you and a whip in close quarters. Other horses are too far away to control at 30 feet but learn better at 10 feet. You will have to experiment. Refer to the free longeing turning sequence for body language and other aids.

Using a Halter

Although a halter is not the best choice of headgear for longeing, it is commonly used! After all, a halter is inexpensive, the horse is usually already accustomed to wearing one, and nylon halters are easily washable. But for a halter to be an effective and safe piece of longeing equipment, it must fit fairly snug so it will not shift. The hardware must not contact the cheekbones or cause rubbing. Since there is not much impact on a horse 30 feet away when he is wearing just a halter, many people use a chain over the horse's nose to increase control. But a chain is not appropriate for longeing. A bosal would be a better choice; a cavesson, an even

---

LONGE LINE GOALS

Whoa on long line.

Walk.

Walk-to-halt transition.

Look at me; don't necessarily face me, but pay attention.

Turn to the inside with longe line.

Walk-to-trot (or jog) transition.

Working trot.

Trot-to-walk transition.

Trot-to-canter transition.

Working canter.

Canter-to-trot transition.

Lengthened trot.

Spiral in and out at the trot and canter.

Canter to walk and walk to canter.

Canter to whoa.

(See *101 Longeing and Long Lining Exercises* for specific line longeing exercises and instructions.)

---

better choice. Once a horse has learned good longeing manners, even longeing with a bridle is better than longeing with a halter. A halter is the least effective head-gear for longeing.

Using a Bosal

A properly fitted bosal with rope fiador, as described in the tack chapter, makes a good longeing headpiece. It is especially good for slowing down and stopping a horse. That's because the longe line is attached at the rear of the bosal, or the heel knot, so that when the longe line is tugged, pressure is exerted on the nose of the horse. This signal is similar to the halter pressure the horse has known since early halter training, only much stronger, so the bosal has good "whoa power." There is no reason a horse can't be longed in a bosal all the time once he has accepted the program. If the horse is at a stage where he might fight or try to pull away, however, you might find that the bosal delivers some nasty skin rubs on the nose and jawbones when the horse jerks or pulls against the pressure on the longe line. It would be better to use a cavesson until the horse accepts the longeing process, and then you can switch to a bosal if you want.

Adding a Cavesson

Before you attempt to longe your horse in a cavesson, review some in-hand work with the horse wearing the cavesson and the line attached to the middle ring on the noseband.

Also, review the turning lessons that your horse received on the long line with a halter. When using a cavesson, you can attach the longe line to the side ring on the noseband or to the center ring. If you use the side ring, you will have to change the point of attachment each time you change direction. At first the sensation of the weighted nosepiece is unfamiliar and the horse might raise his head or freeze. Let him slowly become accustomed to the feel and find his way around.

First Cavesson Lesson— Four-Year-old Trakehner/ QH Filly "A"

Before I send her out for her first cavesson lesson, I ask her to relax and focus by reviewing some head handling (Photo 6.31). She enjoys the attention and melts during the head handling.

6.31

By using gentle waves in the line and the voice command "Eeeeasy," I help her relax and come into a rounder frame, even though her stride remains strong and long (Photo 6.33). But that's OK because this is a productive gait and frame.

6.32

As soon as she begins to move forward, however, it's at an energetic and reaching canter with a bit of a hollow topline (Photo 6.32).

When, with a tug on the line, I ask her to slow down to a trot she acts startled at the pressure on her nose and elevates her head, hollows her back, and trots with short and animated strides.

6.33

On her own, she finds a calmer trot and lowers her whole frame and reaches forward with her head and neck (Photo 6.34). This gives her back a good stretch. This basically was her only initial reaction followed by acceptance.

6.34

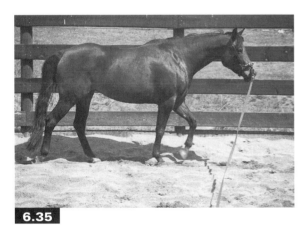

6.35

Filly "B," a half-sister, also a four-year-old Trakehner/QH filly, immediately accepted the cavesson during her first lesson as if she had been worked in it quite a bit already. She is calm, confident, and has a relaxed form (Photo 6.35).

Fitting the Young Horse With a Bridle

There should be only a few new sensations when you bridle a horse for the first time. His ears and head have been handled since birth, he's learned to lower his head from poll pressure, and he opens his mouth for deworming. Bit selection and bridle adjustment are critical, as discussed in Chapter 5.

Hold early bridling lessons in a familiar place, such as the horse's stall or the grooming area. The horse should be untied and standing in a balanced position. Slip the halter off the horse's head and buckle it around his neck. Lay the lead rope across your left arm so you can grab onto it if necessary. Holding the crown-piece of the bridle in your right hand and the bit in your left hand, present the bridle to your horse's face without bumping his

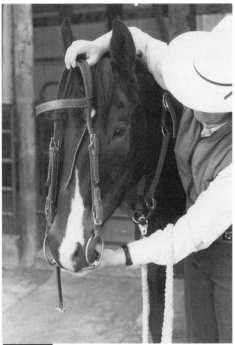

6.36

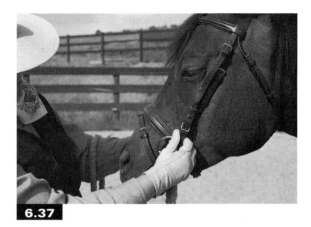

6.37

SIDE REIN GOALS

Move forward into contact.

Lateral bending.

Spiral in and out at regular trot.

Spiral in and out at regular canter.

Canter-to-walk transition.

Walk-to-canter transition.

Canter to Whoa.

Improve and vary gaits.

Flexion.

Begin work on collected gaits.

(See *101 Longeing and Long Lining Exercises* for specific bridle, surcingle, and side rein exercises and instructions.)

eyes or his teeth (Photo 6.36). Place the thumb of your left hand in the interdental space, which will cause the horse to open his mouth. Once the bit is in place, slip the browband over the off ear, and then the near ear. Buckle the throatlatch.

As you check adjustment and fit, be sure the bit is centered in the horse's mouth and that the headstall sits symmetrically on the horse's head (Photo 6.37). Since this is the first bridling for Filly "B," I am taking extra time to see that everything fits properly. She is so relaxed with the procedure that she is dozing.

Leading with a Bridle

Leading a bridled horse is somewhat different from leading a haltered horse. With a lead rope you have one rope that is attached to a ring under the jaw of the horse and you direct the horse with left, right, and backward movements of the rope. A bridled horse has a rein attached to each side of the bit, so if you grab the reins together and treat them as though they were a single lead rope, you give some confusing and contradictory signals to the horse's mouth. Instead, separate the reins with your index finger and use the reins independently to indicate to your horse whether he should turn right or left or slow down (Photo 6.38). If you are using just one line, attach it above the mouthpiece of the bit on the near side so that an upward tug is like a signal for a half halt.

Longeing with or from a bridle is a major step. Everything might have been going smoothly up to this point, so don't get overconfident or careless now. This is

a serious undertaking. Done correctly, adding the bridle to the longeing process provides you with the opportunity to teach your horse many important concepts, such as flexion, bending, and balance. If you approach it haphazardly, however, you could cause a horse pain and injury or cause him to learn bad habits, such as opening his mouth, chewing the bit, or

6.38

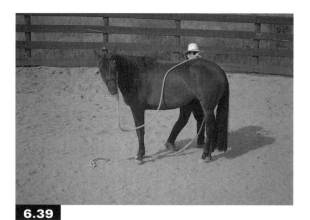

6.39

putting his tongue over the bit or out the side of his mouth. So proceed carefully.

Before you longe your horse with a bridle or from a bridle, you should review the bending exercises that you performed with the halter and cavesson. (Refer to photos 6.20 through 6.25) Now, snap the line to the ring of the snaffle and drape the rope over the horse's body on the opposite side from where you are standing (Photo 6.39). Filly "B" is already thinking about turning left, just from the weight of the rope on the left bit ring.

The first time you ask for bend from the bridle, just ask for a 90- to 180-degree turn. Instead of standing on the opposite side of the horse, stand behind the horse and give a low, soft pull to the line. Sometimes the horse will lock up and push into the unfamiliar, steady pressure on his mouth. Apply light intermittent tugs on the line to break the lock up. Be sure to perform the exercise from both sides. In this case, you will need to change the point of attachment from left bit ring to right bit ring each time you change direction. Work until the horse is comfortable with the pressure and moves forward and bends down long and low into the turn. You might have to perform the exercise over a dozen times in each direction until you get soft compliance. It is time well spent.

Methods of Attaching the Longe Line to the Bridle

The most common, but not necessarily the best or recommended, method of attaching the longe line to the bridle, is to run the longe line through the inside ring, over the poll, and attach it to the outside ring (Photo 6.40). This is a severe method of attachment that magnifies the gentlest signal from the longe line, changing it to quite a severe message. This means of attachment acts like a gag bit. Every time you tug on the longe line, the line shortens, creates pressure on the poll, and raises

6.40

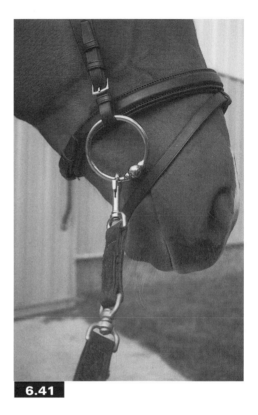

6.41

the bit up in the horse's mouth, basically causing it to act as a gag snaffle. This should be used by experienced trainers only.

Attaching the line to the inside ring of the bit is okay for horses who are well schooled in longeing and no longer do any pulling or bolting (Photo 6.41). If an in-experienced horse pulled, however, it's possible he could pull the bit right through his mouth.

A better setup for a horse in training is to attach the line (the white one in this photo) to both the inside bit ring and the halter cheek ring or to the inside bit ring and the cavesson (Photo 6.42). This will prevent strong pulls and jerks from harming the horse's mouth; however, this requires a longe line with a strap rather than a snap on the end.

6.42

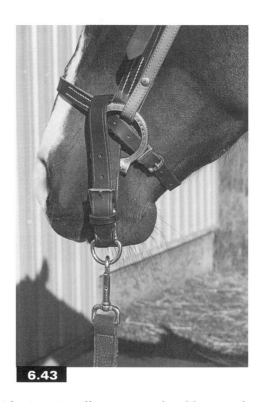

6.43

For longe lines that have a snap on the end, use a longeing strap that buckles to the bit ring and the noseband. The line is snapped to the D-ring on the longeing strap. Here it is shown with a Western bridle and noseband. (Photo 6.43) This distributes the pull between the bit and noseband, protects the horse's mouth, and protects engraved bits from being scratched by the metal snap.

If you attach the line through the inside ring, then under the chin to the outside ring, it will act somewhat like a curb strap. This is more effective at slowing a horse in-hand than it is for keeping him evenly bent on a circle. When the line is pulled, the bit rings come together under the horse's chin, causing the mouthpiece to peak in the horse's mouth and press down at an angle on the bars. This is not a desired action.

Special chin-style longeing straps are also better for a backward pull to slow down a horse in-hand than they are for

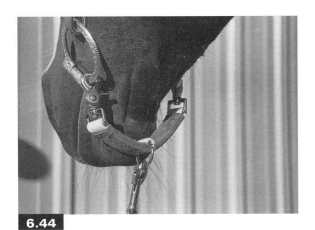

6.44

creating or maintaining bend while longeing (Photo 6.44). If you are using side reins, this type of strap works okay on a well-trained horse.

Introducing Girth Pressure Using a Surcingle or Saddle

In preparation for ground driving and riding, it is desirable to begin shaping the horse and further developing his longitudinal and lateral flexion. Side reins properly attached from either a cavesson or bit to a surcingle or saddle are helpful aids for stretching, conditioning, and suppling exercises.

A horse who has worn a stable or winter blanket is already partly accustomed to the sensations of something on his back and around his girth. Introducing the horse to the pressure of a girth via surcingle or saddle, however, should be a separate lesson held in the confines of a training pen. If you make the mistake of putting a surcingle on your horse in the crossties of your barn, you might end up with quite a wreck on your hands because many horses have an exaggerated reflex reaction to girth pressure the first few times.

First Surcingle Lesson— Four-Year-Old Trakehner/QH Filly "A"

You may want to have an assistant help you with the first lesson in surcingle tacking. The horse is groomed and tacked with a cavesson. Review "sacking out" and let the horse smell and inspect the surcingle. Place the blanket and surcingle gently in position (Photo 6.45). Peak the saddle blanket in the gullet to prevent pressure on the withers when you tighten the surcingle.

Fasten the girth. (If you are using a Western saddle instead of a surcingle, always

6.45

fasten the front cinch first, then the breast collar [if used], and finally the rear cinch. To remove the saddle, unbuckle in the reverse order.) Be sure the girth or cinch is tight enough to prevent the saddle or surcingle from slipping under the horse's belly if she runs or bucks.

Let the horse stand for a few moments, until she has relaxed somewhat. Tighten the girth a bit more. Many accidents occur from a too-loose girth or cinch that allows the surcingle or saddle to slip back or roll under the horse's belly.

Then untrack the horse (get her to step forward), taking care to stand well to her side in the event she lunges forward in a reaction to the girth pressure (Photo 6.46). If she seems rooted to the spot, you can untrack her by turning her head to the right. This will cause her to take one step to the right, then you can head forward. After walking for several minutes in-hand, send the horse out on the longe line at the walk (Photo 6.47). Keep things quiet until you sense that the horse has let out the breath she has been holding!

When you feel it is time, often after just a round or two at the walk, ask the horse to trot. The horse will understandably be more alert than usual because of the new pressure around her middle.

Some horses on their own will break into a canter from the trot and add bucking (Photo 6.48). Discourage bucking. A jerk on the longe line often causes the bucking horse to load the forehand and kick out with the hind legs, which is worse than bucking. A better way to deal with the bucking is to strongly drive the horse forward. This encourages the horse to stretch out rather than curl up. Some trainers hold that a horse should be "bucked out"; that is, the horse should be allowed

6.46

6.47

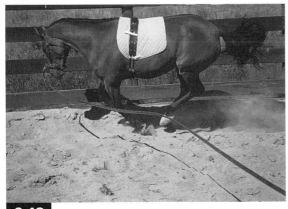

6.48

to buck until she gets it out of her system. I feel that a series of transitions is the best way to help the horse get used to the sensations of girth pressure. Within a few minutes, the surcingle is old stuff. Check the cinches periodically throughout the work to ensure that they are safely adjusted.

Adding a Bridle

Tack the horse up with a bridle, cavesson, surcingle, and longe line and work the horse from the cavesson. Review all the longeing maneuvers the horse has learned through previous longeing methods. At first, some horses are reluctant to move forward energetically while wearing a bridle. You may need to go back to the concentric circle configuration and actively drive the horse forward. It will take a while for the horse to get back to the relaxed state and good form and carriage he had in previous phases of longeing. He might revert to high-head, short-stride, and hollow-back configuration until he becomes accustomed to the bridle. You might need to work the horse for several sessions tacked up this way before you consider adding side reins.

Use of Side Reins with Longeing

Side reins help to balance a moving horse from left to right and begin to introduce contact with the bit. Side reins should always be adjusted to a length that invites and allows the horse to make an actual physical effort to reach for contact with the bit. The side reins should *never* be so short that the horse cannot get momentary relief from contact with the bit without overflexing.

Go slowly with the addition and adjustment of side reins. Allow a horse to gradually get used to the restriction and contact.

Although it seems obvious that a good horseman would never attach side reins to a horse who is in a pen or stall as an attempt to "develop a head set," I've seen enough of this to feel I must include strong advise against it. Using side reins for prolonged periods on an immobile horse only serves to teach the horse to avoid the bit by getting behind it—an extremely hard habit to overcome.

Side reins should not be attached to the horse's headgear or surcingle when the horse is tied or being led. If the side reins are snapped to the saddle or surcingle for leading, when you're leading through doorways and gateways, the loops can catch and cause accidents. I prefer to carry the side reins to the training site.

Always warm up a horse before attaching side reins. After a horse is warmed up, walk out to the horse on the perimeter of the longe circle. Attach the outside rein first, then quickly attach the inside rein and ask the horse to begin moving forward. Step back to the center of the longe circle as he begins walking forward. Side rein adjustment is dependent on the gait so when it comes time to trot or canter, the side reins will need to be shortened. During the cool-down walk, the side reins should be lengthened. Remove side reins when the work is complete and the horse is being led back to the barn.

Side reins are not designed to be used while riding. During a longe lesson with a well-schooled horse, however, side reins can be used as long as a competent professional supervises the session.

The Benefits of Using Side Reins

Side reins accomplish many objectives. For example, they:

- Make the horse focus ahead, where he is going, not to one side or the other.

- Minimize the horse's ability to move his head left or right and can limit to some extent his ability to move his head up and down.

- Allow the trainer to introduce light contact to the horse and to progressively add more contact as the horse develops.

- Encourage a horse to reach forward and down for the bit because the back is unburdened by a rider's weight. This is "finding the bit."

- Encourage a horse to develop balance and self-carriage as the reins *gradually* compact his frame.

- Help control a fresh horse who might otherwise buck and play. Caution must be used when attaching side reins to a fresh horse, and the horse must already have lots of experience with side reins.

You have many choices as to where you can attach side reins. The goal is to eventually use the side reins at a level that approximates a straight line between the horse's mouth and the eventual rider's hands. To reach that stage, however, you will have to use varying positions on the surcingle or saddle to help the horse develop his movement and carriage, and to accommodate the level of his head.

Generally, you start with long, low attachments to encourage the horse to work long and low, then ultimately progress to a shorter and higher attachment point.

Whether you use a surcingle, English saddle, or Western saddle, the girth or cinch should be adjusted symmetrically so that it comes up to an even height on both sides. That way the side reins will be attached at an even height at both sides.

Attaching side reins to a surcingle

Basic position. Lower ring on surcingle (Photo 6.49).

To encourage the horse to lower his head and neck. Just above billet buckles (with or without girth loops).

6.49

To emphasize long and low. Between front legs to girth rings (see Photo 6.55).

Intermediate collection stage. Middle rings on surcingle.

Advanced collection stage. Top rings on surcingle.

Attaching side reins to an English saddle

Basic position. To the girth just above the saddle pad loops; may need to use girth loops; usually results in a horizontal line to horse's mouth (Photo 6.50).

For younger horse, to encourage lower head carriage. Below the pad loops,

may need to use a girth loop (Photo 6.51).

For a schooled horse who doesn't come up above the bit or invert his neck. To the breast collar D-rings (Photo 6.52).

For sliding side reins. combination of breast collar D-rings and girth loops (refer to Chapter 5, Photo 5.28).

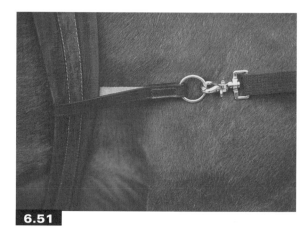

6.51

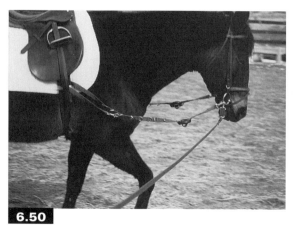

6.50

6.52

Attaching side reins to a Western saddle

Basic position. To the rigging ring (Photo 6.53).

To encourage lower head carriage. To the cinch ring (Photo 6.54).

To work the horse long and low. Between the front legs to the cinch D-rings (Photo 6.55).

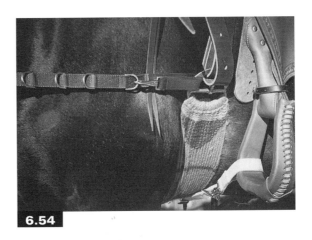

6.54

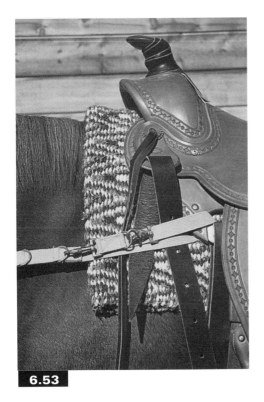

6.53

6.55

6.56

6.57

Intermediate collection position. To the breast collar D-rings (Photo 6.56).

Advanced collection position. Through the gullet to the horn, with reins snapped together (Photo 6.57).

Advanced collection position when using riding reins. Through the gullet and around the horn with a half hitch (Photo 6.58).

6.58

Side Rein Progression

Although it's possible to introduce the idea of side reins by using a halter, a cavesson is a much better piece of equipment because of its effectiveness, stability, and weight. Side reins should be used on the cavesson until the horse becomes accustomed to their feel. Later, they can be used on the bit. With some cavessons, you can snap the side reins to the outer rings on the noseband. If that will not work well, however, you will have to improvise. Make a connector strap or cord that can be attached to the ends of the metal noseband of the cavesson or to the end of the side reins.

First let the horse carry the bridle during longe lessons with very loose rein attachments. Over several lessons, adjust the side reins to create more contact with the cavesson to help the horse learn balance and rounding.

First Side Rein Lesson— Four-Year-old Trakehner/ QH Filly "A"

At first the side reins are adjusted quite long so the four-year-old filly can gradually become accustomed to their restriction. They are long enough to allow her to stretch forward, but they are also long enough to allow her gallop and counterflex (Photo 6.59)! This is not productive. Other typical reactions when contact from side reins is first "felt" by the horse include raising the head, inverting the topline, twisting the head off to one side, hollowing, and moving with short, choppy strides.

The first reaction to a tug on the line might be regressive behavior, such as an attempt to turn toward the rail, but the inside side rein usually puts enough pressure on the horse's nose to discourage that. As with all other phases of longeing, use the "Whoa" and "Stand" to calm the horse and let her relax (Photo 6.60).

If you feel the horse has so much rein that it is causing her to play, you can shorten both side reins. The shorter contact often causes the horse to elevate in front and work with more engagement. This is good. When the filly is asked to trot, this time with slightly shorter side reins, she does so energetically but with a fairly round topline for her first side rein lesson (Photo 6.61).

6.59

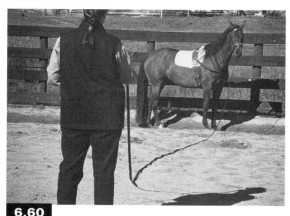

6.60

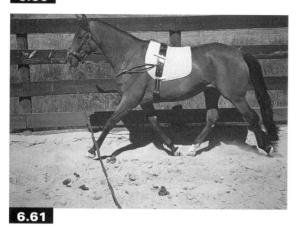

6.61

After ten minutes of work, the side reins are shortened again, the filly is trotted, and then walked, which shows she has accepted the restriction (Photo 6.62). The filly is immediately stopped and the side reins are lengthened. This work with the cavesson will greatly minimize trauma and potential problems when side reins are introduced with the bridle.

First Lesson with Side Reins and Bridle—Filly "B"

For purposes of demonstration, I give Filly "B" her first lesson with a bridle and side reins in a manner I see often but don't recommend: the longe line over the poll, side reins attached to the lower ring on the surcingle (or the girth of the saddle). It's clear that this normally unflappable filly has lots to think about, and she shows her concern with an inverted (hollow) top-line, elevated head, face 35 degrees in front of the vertical, and short, choppy strides (Photo 6.63). After a few minutes work to the right, I change the longe line over her poll and work her to the left, and she begins to improve her movement and form (Photo 6.64). Her length of stride increases and her topline begins rounding slightly.

6.62

6.63

6.64

Since I have a round pen, I often switch back and forth between free longeing and longeing with a line. Often when I introduce a new item of tack to a horse, I use free longeing so the horse has less to think about. I remove the longe line, lower the point of attachment of the side reins, and tighten them slightly. Although this still allows the filly to move freely, it does give her the first "taste" of contact and she reacts by twisting her head from side to side (Photo 6.65). If it looks like just a temporary "testing of the limits," as it was with this filly, let the horse figure out the boundaries. But if it looks as though it could develop into a pattern of behavior, you might want to lengthen the side reins and let the horse just "carry" the bit for a few more.

The aim is to have the horse move actively forward and gradually assume a more balanced and productive working form. The front end should stay somewhat elevated to allow the hindquarters to move actively forward. The topline should be rounded.

Filly B, like most young horses, carries her nose 30 degrees or more in front of the vertical (Photo 6.66). Throughout all of her early work, she should be allowed to carry her nose in this configuration.

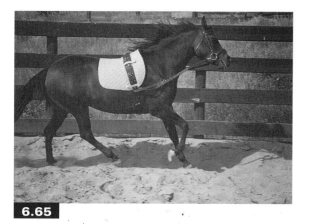

6.65

6.66

6.67

The head and neck are the counter-balance of the hindquarters. As the horse gets stronger in the loin and croup, she will be able to carry more weight with the hindquarters and consequently elevate her head and flex more at the poll. At the end of several months in training, some horses willingly carry themselves with the face line five to ten degrees in front of the vertical, but this is the absolute maximum degree of vertical flexion that should be required/allowed of a developing horse. Prematurely asking a horse to work at or near the vertical may result in a false headset, without the horse developing the much more important aspect of forward movement from the hindquarters. And what's worse, the horse could learn to overflex and get behind the bit, one of the most difficult habits to overcome. Do not let this happen!

Side Rein Adjustment

A horse requires and can tolerate shorter side reins when working at a trot and canter than when working at a walk. The trot and canter both have moments of suspension that allow the horse to regularly round up his topline, which interestingly lengthens the distance along the top of the spine from the poll to the tail but actually shortens the distance from the hock to the mouth. This means the "frame" is compacted but the topline is elongated, which is the ultimate goal of the horse's development: collection.

Side reins should never be used excessively tight to fight a horse or to master him by enforcing cruel submission.

This horse is 30 degrees behind the vertical and his poll has dropped way below the topline of his neck (Photo 6.67). This is very harmful and is only demonstrated for a moment on a patient and forgiving horse to show what not to do! Even if a horse tries to pick his head up with too-short side reins, he can't, so he learns to avoid contact with the bit.

Even if a more appropriate side rein length is restored, a horse who has been worked on too-short reins will tend to back away from the bit and drop his poll. These are both extremely difficult habits to change, so be sure you do not cause them in the first place.

A too-long side rein, on the other hand, accomplishes nothing (Photo 6.68). It may be appropriate for warm-up and cool-down for experienced horses, but a long rein like this can be dangerous if the horse suddenly puts his head down to rub and gets a leg over the rein (Photo 6.69). A too-long or too-rubbery rein can invite a horse to play and root into the bridle, which can be an arm-wrenching problem for a rider to deal with (Photo 6.70).

Shortening of side reins may span a year or more as the horse's condition improves and physique develops. Be careful how long you work a horse with a newly shortened length of rein. When you ride,

6.68

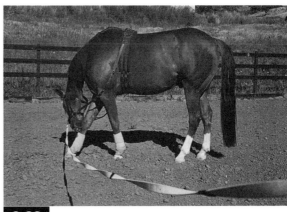

6.69

6.70

you *feel* when it is time to give your horse a break from the constraints of the new degree of connection; but when you are longeing, you may easily miss the visual signs of fatigue. Therefore, only work a horse for a few minutes at shortened rein intensity before offering him the opportunity to stretch his neck and back. Then resume the new contact. Always end the session with a stretch break.

Your side rein work has been correct if the horse:

- Moves forward energetically.

- Has a swinging back.

- Has a swinging tail.

- Moves straight forward.

- Holds his head about 10 to 20 degrees in front of the vertical.

- Gradually develops a rounder, more uphill posture.

Your side rein work has been incorrect if the horse:

- Works on his forehand.

- Is behind the vertical.

- Throws his head up and holds it 40 degrees or more in front of the vertical.

- Has a tense, hollow back.

- Rushes.

- Is short-strided.

- Bolts or rears.

Adjustment of the Inside and Outside Reins

On a circle 20 meters (66 feet) in diameter, for a young horse, the pressure on both reins should be virtually even. Fastening the inside rein shorter asks a degree of bend in the head and neck inappropriate for a young horse in a large circle. Leaving the outside rein too loose may cause the horse to lean on the inside rein and not be able to find the outside rein. This will make the horse fall to the inside of the circle.

As a horse's training progresses, the inside rein is often adjusted shorter than the outside rein. But before I start making adjustments, I often perform a simple suppling and familiarization exercise with very elastic reins, on a small circle, for just a few moments at a time. I fasten the inside rein considerably shorter than the outside rein. I just want the horse to know he can follow his nose around in a small circle (Photo 6.71). You don't want to do this more than a few times for a few moments each time because you could cause your horse to swing his hindquarters out of the

6.71

circle and bulge his shoulder. This horse is bending his body beautifully and stepping under himself deeply. Use this exercise to further fireproof your horse.

For work on large (20-meter) circles, the side reins are used nearly equal in length. Check to be sure that the side reins themselves are equal in length: that is, that one has not been stretched or broken so it is a different length from the other and that the adjustment holes are in exactly the same place. For work on smaller circles, the inside rein can be fastened from one to three holes shorter than the outside rein. This allows the horse to gently bend into the direction of the circle and also enables the horse to take contact with the outside rein. Such an adjustment will help a horse find his balance. Every time a horse moves with an irregular or quick rhythm he is telling you he has momentarily lost his balance and is scurrying to find it.

The outside rein is a stabilizing force that keeps the outside shoulder straight and prevents it from bulging out of the circle. A horse worked with a too-tight inside rein and a too-loose outside rein will likely overbend to the inside and consequently bulge his outside shoulder and possibly move his hindquarters out of the circle. An increased outside rein contact will help to keep the outside shoulder in under the horse.

If a horse is very stiff when going to the right, for example, he may pull against the shorter right rein and bend to the left, even if he is being worked on a circle to the right. This stiffness is a result of the left side of the horse's body being stronger than the right. In a situation like this, at first the outside rein may have to be loosened and the inside rein positioned as low as possible and tightened a bit more. This would be just "to show" the horse that he can bend right. If the horse is explosive or very inexperienced, however, this type of remedy can get you in trouble. That's why I like the close-in, low-key circling exercise in the previous photo—you are showing the horse the same thing—he can follow his nose in both directions.

If a horse falls to the inside, or overbends in one direction, loosen the inside rein and tighten the outside rein to hold him up on the perimeter of the circle. Holding longeing lessons in a round pen is a great aid to help you contain the horse's body and help prevent leaning, stiffening,

and counterflexing without overusing contact with side reins.

Spiral Exercise— Experienced Quarter Horse Gelding

As your horse becomes more experienced with side reins, you can begin more collected work. Spiraling a horse in and out at a canter is a tremendous exercise for introducing collection for brief periods of time.

Establish the canter on a 20-meter circle, paying attention to rhythm and form (Photo 6.72). Your goal is to maintain the same rhythm of the canter, no matter what the size of the circle. Also, you want to be sure that the horse's poll remains the highest point of his frame and that his hindquarters stay well engaged.

The line is shortened to a 15-meter circle while the whip stays in an active position to keep the gelding cantering in a smaller circle (Photo 6.73). The trainer is in essentially the same spot.

On a 10-meter circle, the gelding maintains his collected frame and rhythm, but the tension on the line tells me that at this time in his training it is as small a circle as he can canter in balance (Photo 6.74). I ask him to canter for only two circles at 10 meters.

I gradually let him out by stepping toward him and using an active driving whip. I let the line slip through my hands while maintaining good contact with the line. A horse often needs a bit of help balancing on the spiral out.

The line is let out to a 15-meter circle; the horse is worked for two circles and gradually returns to the 20-meter circle in the same form as he began (Photo 6.75).

6.72

6.74

6.73

6.75

Longeing the Trained English Horse Prior to Riding

Once your horse is proficient at longeing, you may want to use it only for warming him up prior to riding. You can tack him up for riding with the modifications described next (Photo 6.76).

6.76

6.77

With the reins in riding position, twist them a couple of times and then take one rein and buckle it into the throatlatch to keep the reins out of the way (Photo 6.77).

The stirrups can be tied with a simple overhand knot in the leathers to keep them from flapping (Photo 6.78).

Another method of securing the stirrups involves wrapping the leathers around the tread and lacing the end of the stirrup leather through the bottom loop (Photo 6.79).

If you are going to be longeing for a long time or if the stirrups might scratch the saddle, you can use soft, fleece stirrup

6.78

pockets to hold the stirrups in position and protect the saddle (Photo 6.80).

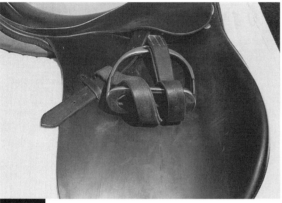
6.79

6.80

Problems and Solutions

Young horses as well as experienced horses will have problems on the longe line. Many problems on the longe line have the same causes as problems during in-hand work and riding. Here are some of the most common solutions to horse behavior problems in general:

Make sure the horse has plenty of regular, free exercise.

Be sure he is only being fed the grain he requires for his workload. Check to be sure that the horse is not receiving too much high-energy feed.

Be sure all tack has been introduced to the horse in a systematic fashion.

Make sure all tack is clean and well fitted.

Drive the horse forward—this eliminates many problems.

PROBLEM *Anticipation*—the horse takes off when you first arrive in the training area or he reacts during the session before you ask a change from him.

SOLUTION Once a horse has learned what is coming, he may do what he expects will be asked. This is a symptom of a nervous horse or a rushed training program. But it also can be a symptom of a very keen horse who is so "tuned in" that he gets into trouble! To prevent anticipation, vary the sequence of the lesson maneuvers, the location of the lessons, and keep things moving forward in a progression.

PROBLEM   *Playfulness*—the horse runs, bucks, and does not pay attention, or he throws his head and plays instead of paying attention. This can be dangerous to the horse's legs and back as well as to the handler.

SOLUTION   The horse needs to be turned out for exercise before longeing. Never take a horse who has been cooped up in a stall or small pen and expect him to pay attention and learn a new lesson. Be sure you have all equipment adjusted so that it is effective. A too-long, too-stretchy side rein invites a horse to play. Give a playful horse something else to think about—drive him actively forward.

PROBLEM   *Disobedience*—the horse cannot be stopped, wraps himself in the longe line, whirls, is willful, kicks, or otherwise misbehaves (Photo 6.81).

6.81

SOLUTION   First, determine whether the horse is afraid of the longe line, the whip, his headgear, or you. If so, go back to the basics of handling and gentling and familiarize your horse with the various articles of tack. Check his headgear to be sure it fits properly and is not causing unwanted pain when pressure is applied. If the horse is simply unfamiliar with the longeing process, often just driving him actively forward will "straighten out" the problem. You may have to temporarily sacrifice rhythm and tempo to at least get the horse going forward.

If you have ruled out fear and unfamiliarity, you will need to review in-hand work and insist on obedience at the walk, trot, and halt. Work the horse in an enclosed area—a round pen the size of your longeing circle is ideal. If you do not have one, use the end of an arena and, if possible, close it off with some portable panels. Take the opportunity to discipline the horse if he is willfully disobedient. The correction in-hand will carry over to the longeing work. If a horse kicks while free longeing, immediately turn him hard into the fence (rollback) twice so he is then traveling in the same direction he was initially. Act as if nothing has happened. If he kicks again, repeat. If a horse kicks on the longe line, use the cavesson to immediately discipline him and turn him into the circle. If the problem continues, seek the help of a professional who might choose to use a different type of headgear for that particular horse.

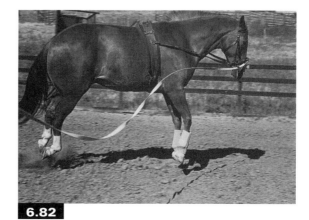

6.82

PROBLEM *Bucking*—the horse crow-hops, rounds his back, tucks his croup, and bogs his head (Photo 6.82).

SOLUTION If the horse is very fresh and bucks when you longe him, have you been turning him out often enough and before you longe? If the bucking is a reaction to

girth pressure, be sure the girth is not too tight and does not pinch or have foreign material pressing into the horse's skin. If a horse bucks out of playfulness or freshness, just drive him forward. If a horse bucks out of sheer disobedience, have headgear on him that will allow you to reprimand him sharply when his feet are off the ground. Here's where a chain with a halter might be in order. A well-fitted cavesson usually does the trick.

PROBLEM *Balking*—the horse won't go forward.

SOLUTION Since the cause of freezing is usually fear or uncertainty, if you feel this is why the horse won't move, carefully evaluate the progression you have been following. Sometimes a horse will freeze from the addition of a new piece of tack, such as a cavesson or side reins. If you determine this to be the cause, the solution is remove and review.

A horse who is balking from sullenness is a much more difficult problem to deal with. The sullen horse must be handled by an experienced trainer who knows when to push and when to quit.

PROBLEM *Laziness*—a horse has to be continually prodded to make him move and keep him going.

SOLUTION Check to be sure that he is being fed enough energy feed for his level of work. Be sure you are deworming and vaccinating on a regular basis. A horse with parasites or a respiratory infection will lack initiative. Ensure that a competent farrier regularly cares for the horse's feet. Let the farrier know the surface the horse is being worked on. Sometimes a young horse will require front shoes but most often, if the longeing footing is good, a horse can be barefoot. If the horse's health, nutrition, and hooves all check out

and he still appears lazy, he might just be smart and have learned that he doesn't *have* to work. The kindest yet most effective way to encourage a horse to move out and get in shape is through the use of the whip.

Most of the time, just the sight and sound of the whip cracking will get a horse moving. But if a horse has learned to ignore the whip, you will have to remind him that you can reach him with it. You will need to have a long longe whip with a longe lash. Practice popping the whip ahead of time so that when you aim for the horse's croup or hock, that's what you hit. Usually one well-placed pop will wake up even the laziest horse and get him moving. If you merely come at a horse with a wiggling whip or tap him lightly with it, he will become desensitized to it and you will lose this very important driving aid. It is more humane in the long run—and definitely more effective—to use a whip once, in the correct place and with optimum intensity. With a lazy horse, instead of staying in the center of the circle and pivoting around, you will have to walk a medium-sized concentric circle while the horse works on the larger circle.

PROBLEM *Pulling*—you feel as though you are waterskiing instead of longeing.

SOLUTION If you are longeing in an open area or a large arena and the horse pulls on the line, don't just pull back. This is one tug of war you will definitely lose. Instead, use intermittent tugs or jerks on the line so the horse feels pressure and release. It is something like pumping your brakes to stop your vehicle. Be sure your whip is in a neutral position as you try to regain control. If this happens with a halter, no wonder! Switch to a bosal or cavesson.

PROBLEM *Rushing*—a horse takes short, quick steps.

SOLUTION A horse in a hurry is either afraid or out of balance. Be sure the horse is familiarized with all equipment and does not fear you when doing in-hand work. Work him at the walk and trot only, with lots of transitions. Reduce the circle size if necessary. Carry the whip so you can use it in front of his chest to slow him down. Or turn around and face him to slow him down. He might turn, but eventually he will learn to slow down.

PROBLEM *Wrong lead*—the horse is being worked in a circle to the left and is on the right lead (Photo 6.83). Or the horse is *disunited*; that is, he is cantering on one lead with the front legs and the opposite lead with the hind.

SOLUTION I've found it is the rare horse who takes the wrong lead when being free longed in a 66-foot round pen. As soon as you add a longe line, halter, cavesson, or bridle, however, you are changing that horse's balance. When side reins are not being used, you will see a horse's natural tendency to left-right balance and suppleness. Most horses will take the wrong lead occasionally but will usually take the correct lead when brought back to a trot and

6.83

asked again for canter. If a horse consistently takes the wrong lead in a particular direction, he is exhibiting stiffness. With a horse like that, it would be best to wait until you introduce side reins before working on the lead problem. Although side reins can help to develop suppleness and left-right balance and teach a horse to take the correct lead, if side reins are used too early or improperly, they can actually teach the horse to take the wrong lead at the canter. For example, if your horse is tracking left and you have a tighter inside side rein to try to "make" the horse bend to the left, the horse may very likely take the right lead when asked to canter. The same horse, with head left free, quite likely will hold his head off to the right and take the left lead!

At first, the disunited horse can be treated in the same manner as the horse who takes the wrong lead: downward then upward transition. I usually move a disunited horse forward with strong aids for a moment, however, and that usually causes the horse to "unite." It's as if the horse were "popped" into synchronization. If you feel the horse would be frightened and rush uncontrollably from strong driving aids, it might be better to bring the horse back to a trot or walk and then reestablish the canter, hopefully on the correct lead and united.

PROBLEM The horse *changes leads* while longeing.

SOLUTION Sometimes a horse will strike off on the correct lead because of your impeccable timing of aids (or luck!) and then switch to the wrong lead. Frustrating! This is usually because the horse is tired, lame, or stiff. If he has been worked to the left quite a bit during a particular session, for example, it would not be surprising for him to seek relief from the left lead by switching to the right lead. If the horse is lame, of course, even though his training reflexes have him take the correct lead for a few steps, his self-preservation will kick in and he will switch because it hurts. The solution for those two situations is to quit the session and take the appropriate health-care steps. For the horse who switches leads because he is stiff, it may be too early in his training and conditioning to canter. Period. You might need to go back to lots of walk-trot transitions with side reins until the horse has learned to bend equally in both directions.

PROBLEM   *Boredom*—horse is tuned out, listless.

SOLUTION   Avoid boredom by not overdoing longeing. Don't work the horse too long too many times per week. And be sure to keep variety in the session. All too often longeing is used to tire a horse out, and the horse is cantered for long periods of time with no transitions or change of direction. Your horse should always be listening and watching you. If he ignores commands, performs upward or downward transitions when he feels like it, and is basically tuned out, you will have to go back to the body language portion of the free longeing section to get the horse's attention. Assess the use of your voice commands and body language and be sure they are appropriate, consistent, and are being used with enough intensity. Then ask nicely once—and, if you are ignored—back up your request with an appropriately forceful aid. Do not use a command over and over again once the horse is doing what is asked. It is not necessary to continue to

say "Trot, trot" once the horse, is trotting. This may dull him to your transition commands. Keep cues sparse and effective. Change the area you longe in to vary the environment. This will wake up most horses, but could possibly result in the horse paying more attention to his new surroundings than to you will. Control is always a problem when you longe in an open area. Introduce a new or more advanced aspect to the horse's routine longeing lessons. Possibilities include a gait extension, collection, longeing over a few ground rails, working on irregular terrain, and longeing with side reins and a surcingle or a saddle.

PROBLEM   *Cutting corners*—the horse shaves one side off the circle, making a flat spot. Or the horse won't work full out on the longe line but wants to work close to you.

SOLUTION   Here is one habit you want to be sure to nip in the bud. When a horse does not track a perfect circle but rather makes one portion flat, he is not receiving any of the benefits of working on a circle and he is learning that he can take control. To prevent a horse from cutting into the circle, take a giant step toward him while sending a wave through your longe line to pop him on the shoulder and at the same time aim the whip at his hindquarters. In this case, you are using the whip as a visual aid, so you can use it as though you were fencing—en garde, lunge! You might want to incorporate a command like "Go on" or "Get out there." Never compensate for your horse's irregular circle by backing up when he travels closer to the center. Instead, make him move out and take contact with the longe line. Side reins, with the outside rein adjusted slightly tighter, will help keep a horse on the track of the longeing circle.

PROBLEM   *Shying*—veering or jumping sideways at real or imagined things.

SOLUTION   Sometimes a horse will veer in because he is spooking at something unfamiliar outside the pen. Take the time to review in-hand work and build up your horse's confidence by working him near and over obstacles. If he is playing or making up boogie men, use the techniques outlined in the preceding section on cutting corners.

PROBLEM   *Unbalanced or stiff movement*—the horse does not bend when traveling in a circle.

SOLUTION   It is okay if a young horse carries himself straight on a 20-meter circle. Once the horse gains some experience, however, he should start lowering and bending inward. If you see that a horse carries himself stiff to the outside, with his head up or his back hollow, you'd be better off postponing his longeing lessons until he's at an age where you can introduce side reins and a surcingle or use ground driving. If you let a horse repeat stiff circles over and over again with poor carriage and movement, these habits will not only carry over in his memory patterns but also will train his body to develop in those configurations.

PROBLEM   The horse *turns in* and faces you and either stops or starts walking toward you.

SOLUTION   This is a serious fault to avoid. Unfortunately, many people think that it is "sweet" when a horse wants to come to the trainer. But the horse has basically said one of two things, "I challenge you" or

"I'm not going to work." Your goal is to keep the horse facing forward on the track of the circle and moving forward at all times, except when you want him to turn. When he halts, he should stop on the line of the circle. Make sure you are not causing the horse to turn in by inadvertently getting ahead of him, or stepping backward as you longe, and pulling the line toward you. You should always walk forward as you longe. If a horse further challenges you by charging you, you must lunge toward the horse and back him down; otherwise, this could be a serious problem. When you are using side reins, the outside side rein should be adjusted to help you keep the horse on the track. Be sure the inside rein is not too tight; otherwise, it might be inviting him in.

PROBLEM The horse *turns away* from you.

SOLUTION It is normal for a horse to turn away from you when you first teach him to free longe. If the habit persists even after you have shown him the difference with a longe line, however, you will need to go back to the bending and flexing exercises in-hand. With a cavesson, you can snap the line on the inside ring.

PROBLEM *Rearing*—the horse stands up on his hind legs.

SOLUTION Rearing is a loss of forward motion coupled with an avoidance behavior. The horse is trying to avoid the effect of the aids. Rearing while being longed is almost always caused by too much restriction on the horse, usually from side reins. This is a situation to avoid because it seems that once a horse rears, and perhaps falls over and breaks a piece of equipment, the behavior is more easily repeated. That is why side rein use is an art, and side reins are intended to be introduced gradually and monitored carefully. If side reins are used too short or are attached before the horse is sufficiently warmed up, the horse's top-line can't round into the contact. Rather, the back will hollow and the horse's head will come up, which is an invitation to rearing.

PROBLEM The horse *rolls* when you take him to the round pen.

SOLUTION If possible, keep the round pen and other training areas for training only. If your training pens double as turn-out pens, it is no wonder that a horse who is sometimes led to the pen to be turned out will make that association with the pen when he is taken there to work. Many horses roll as soon as they are turned out; that is just natural horse behavior.

To Avoid Problems

As you work your horse on the longe line, aim to develop his gaits so they are pure and unhurried but have plenty of energy from the hindquarters. If you allow a horse to rush or work with an uneven or impure rhythm, it will carry over to his saddle work. Influencing the tempo of a horse's gaits on the longe line is one of the most difficult aspects of longeing. You must encourage energy and action from the horse, using your body language and the whip, while at the same time containing him with the action of your body and the longe line.

7

LONG LINE TECHNIQUES

Long lining, also called ground driving or long reining, is a continuation of the longeing progression that uses two lines instead of one. That's why it is sometimes also called "double longeing." The two lines are attached to the cavesson or the bridle and the horse is driven in front of the trainer, alongside the trainer in a straight line, or around the trainer in a circle, as in longeing.

Tack for Long Lining

Long Lines

Even though there are some similarities between long lining and longeing, it would be difficult to effectively use two longe lines as a pair of long lines. A good longe line has a substantial snap, a swivel, and leather stops (refer to Chapter 5, Photos 5.1 and 5.2). All of these features would cause problems with the lines flowing through surcingle rings. In a good pair of long lines for long-range work, each line would be 35 feet long, with the last 10 feet sewn round to easily slide through rings, and with a small snap that easily passes through the rings. Long lines for close-up work would be about 18 feet long, with the last 6 feet sewn round.

Long lines can be thought of as long reins that allow you to communicate with a horse's mouth from distances of between 8 to 30 feet. If you plan to perform 20-meter circles or arena maneuvers such as serpentines or figure-eights, you must use lines that are 35 feet long. This will provide enough length for the outside line to go around the horse's side and hindquarters and still be long enough for a 20-meter circle.

Long lines should be a perfect compromise between lightness and heft. The material should be light enough so the lines don't drag heavily on the ground when a horse is working 30 feet away from you. (Any line 30 feet long will sag somewhat.) Heavy lines put an unnecessary pull on the horse's mouth and holding, them can be fatiguing for you as well. Very lightweight lines, however, are often not comfortable to hold and flutter in the breeze.

A hefty long line can be used to pop a lazy horse on the hindquarters. Sisal rope lines have a good snap and firmness but are heavy on the horse's mouth and in the rider's hands and can cause friction burns if a fight ensues. Leather lines, although very expensive, are ideal for close-up long reining if they are not too heavy, but they are too heavy for long-range work. Medium-weight ribbed cotton lines work the best for large circles and arena figures.

The snaps on long lines must be moderately strong yet small enough to pass through conventional surcingle rings. If the snaps (like those on many longe lines) are too large to pass through the surcingle rings, to fasten the lines, you would have to run 30 feet of line through the rings backward. Heavy snaps dangle an unnecessary weight on the horse's mouth.

Surcingle

The surcingle you use for longeing may or may not be suitable for long lining. If the rings stand out from the surcingle in a fairly fixed, rigid configuration, the surcingle should work. Rings that easily flop one way or the other can collapse on a line and trap it, causing an abrupt jerk or lack of flow of the line. The back piece of a conventional surcingle often has large rings on its bottom edge, just above the billets. These rings are often used for the initial stages of long lining.

There are usually two other sets of large rings above the lowest set; they can be used as the horse progresses and his head comes up.

Harness saddles and surcingles specifically designed for long lining have two large metal rings (terrets) that stand in an upright position on top of the back piece (Photo 7.1). Lines are able to pass through terrets more freely than through moveable rings that can collapse onto the line. But because of the high line position, top-terret long lining is the most advanced stage.

Instead of running the lines through the terrets, you can run the lines alongside the terrets when you are working behind the horse. When you step to one side or the other of the horse, the inside line can come straight to your hand while the outside line can run alongside the terret and to your other hand; and when you change direction, you don't have to stop and re-thread any lines.

If a lower point of control is necessary, the reins may be passed through the shaft tugs of a driving harness that are located midway down the horse's ribs. The shaft tugs are leather loops (sometimes metal lined) where the shafts of the cart rest (refer to Photo 7.1).

If a horse has a good set of withers and is not fat, a surcingle should stay in place, provided it is fastened snugly. If you are long lining round or fat ponies or horses with low withers, however, you might want to consider stabilizing the surcingle with a breast collar and/or a crupper (Photo 7.2). The breast collar will keep the surcingle

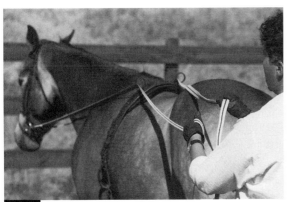

7.1

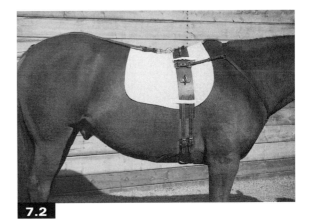

7.2

from shifting rearward. It should be fastened snugly. The crupper consists of a strap that attaches to the surcingle and a loop that fastens under the horse's tail. (Photo 7.3) Many horses will kick or buck when they first feel a crupper under their tail. But since you did a thorough job of desensitizing your horse to ropes under his tail, you should have no problem, right?

If you are going to drive your horse, using an English saddle, you can run the lines through the stirrups to give a nice low pull, good for early lessons (Photo 7.4). You will need to hobble the stirrups under the horse's belly with a stirrup hobble strap (Photo 7.5).

7.4

7.3

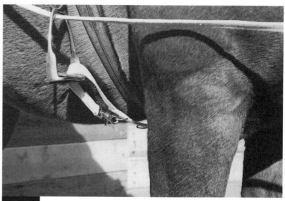

7.5

Benefits of Long Lining

As a matter of course, I conduct all beginning and intermediate long lining lessons first with the lines attached to the side rings on the cavesson. This allows the horse to get used to the presence and action of two lines, to the idea of change of bend and change of rein and direction, and to stopping without bit pressure. Once the horse is comfortable with the routine, the lines can be attached to the bit.

Longeing with side reins introduced the horse to bit presence and contact. Long lining introduces bit action. Long lining not only has similar exercise and training benefits as longeing, but also relates the signals for gait transitions, turns, and halts specifically to the action of the bit and bridle. Long lining can be the definitive cure for a horse who turns to face the trainer or one who cuts off part of the circle, since the outside line will keep the horse straight and on the track.

In fact, it is the communication with the outside line, specifically, that makes long lining such a valuable teaching aid. At first the outside line is used mainly to control the position of the horse's hindquarters. As the training advances, the outside line becomes an active aid for developing contact, bend, and collection. To achieve this, as lessons progress, be aware of any attempt by the horse to stretch into the contact with the outside line. Recognize this, respond to it, and yield when the horse softens and lowers yet retains an active contact with the outside line. Keep the horse actively moving forward. This will be especially helpful in work to the right where the horse does not take contact consistently with the left (outside) rein.

With long lining, for the first time, the horse will feel the movement of your hands on his mouth. Long lines give you a powerful amount of leverage, so be very careful how you use them. Your goal should be to improve and add to the maneuvers that the horse learned in longeing.

Specifically, long lining is well designed to teach halt, backing, bending and turning, and performing changes in direction. Long lining is a valuable means for fine-tuning certain points with intermediate and older horses: bending and flexion, flying changes, and upper-level dressage movements.

For intermediate and more advanced riding horses, sometimes working on a more intricate movement or concept can get tedious or the horse's back can get sore. Working on the maneuver in long lines can be more relaxing, fun, and a change of pace for the horse and trainer, and can give the horse's back a chance to rest and round.

Since you will have two long lines to keep track of, long lining is potentially more dangerous in terms of tangles for both horse and trainer. And since the lines are attached directly to the bit, if an accident does occur, the horse's mouth can easily be injured. After 25 years of long lining, however, I wholeheartedly believe the benefits greatly outweigh the potential risks.

Styles of Long Lining

There are various styles of working a horse from the ground with long lines:

- **ENGLISH**   This is also known as *long lining* by Western trainers. The lines pass through the lower rings of a surcingle, the shaft loops of a driving saddle, or the stirrups of a Western or English saddle. The horse is either driven straight ahead of the trainer (sometimes called "plow driving") or around the trainer in a circle. In the latter situation, the outside rein runs around the horse's hindquarters, resting just above the hocks as the horse works. When a saddle is used, the stirrups are stabilized along the horse's side by hobbling them together under the horse's belly. English long lining is the main method of long lining described in this book.

- **DANISH**   Using a surcingle with top terrets, the reins come to the trainer's hands across the middle of the horse's back. The trainer often walks alongside as she schools the horse on light contact to movements containing higher levels of difficulty. A horse can also be worked in a circle around the trainer, but when using this method the horse must be very experienced; otherwise he could easily turn and face the trainer. This method is demonstrated later in this chapter.

- **FRENCH**   Using a collar and bitting rig with side terrets, the horse is driven from the rear. This method emphasizes a higher head and neck position reminiscent of French carriage horses.

LONG-REINING PROGRESSION

Plow drive with cavesson (consider using an assistant).

Plow drive with cavesson solo.

English drive with cavesson in circle.

Plow drive with bridle.

English drive with bridle in circle.

Optional step: Inside line directly to hand; outside line through lower surcingle ring (must change lines to change direction).

Optional step: Inside line directly to hand; outside line through terret (must change lines to change direction).

Optional step: Inside line directly to hand; outside line running behind terret but not through it (not necessary to change lines when changing direction).

Danish drive with both lines running through top terrets.

(See *101 Longeing and Long Lining Exercises* for specific long lining exercises and instructions.)

- **VIENNESE** Although the horse wears a bitting rig or decorated saddle pad, the reins do not pass through terrets. This method is used to exhibit an already very well-trained horse.

The English method is used for introducing long lining to a horse for the first time. It allows you the best chance for control and provides a low pull to regain control if things get exciting. Because of the very low rein position, however, overuse of this style of long lining can lead to a low head carriage and overbending at the jaw and poll. Once the horse is obedient and controllable, it is best to run the lines through a higher, intermediate set of rings.

Holding and Using Long Lines

For plow driving, the line from the horse comes in the top of the hand and the tail end of the line exits at the bottom of the hand (Photo 7.6). A hold with "feel."

Sometimes you need a "power" hold for working the horse in a circle. The line from the horse comes into the bottom of your hand and out the top (Photo 7.7). The ends of the line are flipped forward, which keeps them out of your way.

When holding both reins in one hand in Photo 7.8, (the right one) your other

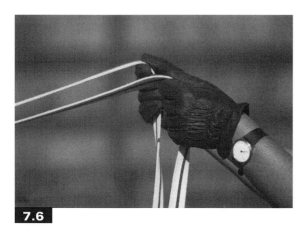

7.6

7.7

7.8

hand (left) can slide forward to aid in shortening the lines.

Unlike your relatively static position when longeing, when long lining you need to actively move around the training arena as you work on the different maneuvers. Usually you will not carry a whip for long lining, but if you do, it is generally in the left hand when the horse is tracking right. In more advanced maneuvers it can be in either hand, depending on whether you want to effect more drive or more bend. The association you made with your voice commands and body language during longeing should create the impulsion you need for long lining. To move a horse forward or out on the circle, you can "cast a wave" in the long lines, aiming at a particular hindquarter, shoulder, or side. This wave should not result in a pull on the bit in the horse's mouth.

Should You Use an Assistant?

Using an assistant to help start a horse long lining is often recommended.

Advantages: Two heads can be better than one; there is safety in numbers; the horse is used to someone working in the in-hand position.

Disadvantages: The assistant must be experienced and confident; you must re-hearse, and for some things you can't; two people can confuse a horse who wonders who he should listen to; the assistant can get in the way or get hurt.

Starting Out and Basic Work

For safety, all long lining should take place in a safe enclosure. The first lesson usu-ally entails tacking up, affixing the lines, stepping a safe distance behind the horse (in the plow-driving position), and asking him to walk forward. Sometimes an assis-tant at the horse's head will give the horse added confidence, and may prevent a wreck; at other times the assistant might get you in trouble.

The "plow-driving" phase of the English/ Western method gives the horse a chance to feel your hands through the lines in an even, balanced position. At this stage, the lines do not cross a moving part of the horse's body, and so are relatively stable and nonfrightening.

Once the walk and halt have been taught, you can step to the side of the horse and send the horse around you, as in longeing. When the horse feels the outside line on the hocks, it should not be alarm-ing if you took the time earlier to famil-iarize him with ropes.

Circles and half turns at the walk and trot are a good introduction to the give and take between the left and right lines. It is important in a change of direction that you allow the rein of the old direction to give way to the rein of the new direction, thereby avoiding conflicting signals.

The figure-eight is a valuable exercise for introducing turning and the change of rein. As you ask for bending with one line, you will have to give with the other to al-low the horse to bend. Depending on the sharpness of the turn and the gait and speed in which the horse is working, the giving can be accomplished by letting the outside line (outside of the turn) slide through your hand, or you may be able to reach your arm forward or lift your arm to provide sufficient give.

When practicing a figure-eight with long lines, at first you will use the lazy X configuration at the center of the figure-eight. The lazy X configuration will allow you to drive your horse on a long straight diagonal line between the two circles of the figure-eight. This will provide ample time for you and the horse to change bend.

If a horse is circling left, the left line is asking him to bend left, and the right line is allowing him to bend left. As he approaches the lazy X, the lines should straighten him out so that when he crosses the center point, he is tracking straight ahead, even on both lines. Then the right line asks for a bend to the right and the left line allows it. If in either direction the horse falls onto the inside shoulder, making the circle on that side of the figure-eight too small, you will have to hold a little more pressure with the outside line to keep the horse up on his outside shoulder. Most horses will try this on one side of the figure-eight and not on the other because of the natural tendency of horses to be one-sided.

Once the Lazy X figure-eight is mastered, you will gradually compact the horse and aim for a perfect equitation pattern figure-eight with the circles just kissing at the center. (See *101 Longeing and Long Lining Exercises* for a variety of figure-eights and changes of rein.)

First Lesson: Filly "A"

Filly "A" has been tacked up with a cavesson and surcingle. The long lines pass through the lowest rings on the surcingle. I'm standing a safe distance behind the filly in the plow-driving position (Photo 7.9). I require her to stand quietly for at least a minute before asking her to walk.

When she begins walking, I immediately give her some slack in the lines to confirm that that was a correct move (Photo 7.10). Because I hold the initial session in the round pen for safety reasons, I must immediately begin turning her in a gentle, large arc.

Later when she shows me she is ready to let me step to her side, I use the outside line (in this case, the left line) to direct her over to the rail (Photo 7.11). My right line is quite slack because I want to make it very clear she is to move to the left, and I don't want any conflicting signals. She is a sensitive filly.

When she is comfortable with the idea of working around me in long lines, I ask her to trot (Photo 7.12). She is moving in an expected form at first: rangy, nose out. The long lines here are a much better

7.9

7.12

7.10

7.11

example of the tension they should have at this stage.

As with all the other phases of groundwork, I place great emphasis on the "Whoa" and "Stand" (Photo 7.13). This gives the horse time to focus and develop patience, and it gives me time to reorganize my lines.

By 15 to 20 minutes into the session, the filly has absorbed the lesson. She accepts the new sensations and responds as solidly as she did in longeing. Her movement is giving me gooseflesh. She has attained a nice uphill form with great impulsion (Photo 7.14). From this point, we are ready to go on!

With most horses, you'd quit here for the first session and be very happy. But I need to take advantage of the good weather for photos, so I will begin the change

7.13

7.14

7.15

of rein lesson. I just want to get her used to the idea of bending, turning, and change of direction. With about 20 feet of line between me and the filly, I bend her left by taking with the left line and giving with the right line (Photo 7.15). She bends in a nice arc to the left. This goes smoothly because she was introduced to the concept of turning on a long line first from a halter and then from the cavesson. (Refer to Chapter 6, Photos 6.20 to 6.25).

First Lesson with Bridle: Filly "B"

Filly "B" is tacked up with a snaffle bridle and surcingle, and the lines are running through the lower rings of the surcingle. We start out in the plow-driving position walking straightforward (Photo 7.16).

I want to be sure I can stop and start her before I ask her to turn or work around me in a circle. To stop her, I say, "Whoa" and then lightly lift up on the lines, maintain my position, and let her walk into the contact, which causes her to stop and stand (Photo 7.17).

When I ask her to start forward again, with a voice command, she is reluctant at first to walk into the light pressure on her

7.16

7.18

7.17

7.19

mouth (the weight of the long lines). So I pitch waves (send slack) in both lines simultaneously, taking care not to pull on her mouth (Photo 7.18). She begins to walk forward before the waves even land on her sides.

When I ask her to turn left by pulling backward on the left line and giving with the right line, she continues moving forward with her head low, which is good,

but I feel a bit of stiffness in her response (Photo 7.19). This is typical. Many horses are confused by the pressure and tend to freeze up or tense.

I find her response much better when I step out to the side and slightly behind her and ask for some left bend with the left line (Photo 7.20). I don't want her to turn sharply inward, so I am maintaining contact on the right line.

7.20

7.21

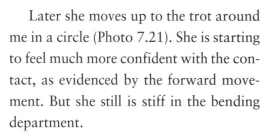

7.22

Later she moves up to the trot around me in a circle (Photo 7.21). She is starting to feel much more confident with the contact, as evidenced by the forward movement. But she still is stiff in the bending department.

When I work her to the left the next time, instead of passing the left line through the surcingle ring, I let the line come straight to my hand so I can have a much more direct inward pull on the corner of her mouth (Photo 7.22). This seems to be a clearer message to her, and she begins to stride out confidently. This is a good place to quit with this horse for the first lesson.

She will require more suppling exercises than Filly "A." I will spend a month practicing various size circles, serpentines, and changes of rein both in and out of the circle.

Backing is an advanced maneuver and is best introduced from the plow-driving position, which will help to ensure straightness in the maneuver. All rein cues should be alternate rein, with intermittent pressure on the bit. With backing, these techniques are paramount. Steady pressure encourages strong resistance. Standing a safe distance behind your horse in the plow-driving position, hold the lines evenly in your hands. Then with the voice command you used with in-hand work ("Baaaack") gently pull one rein and then the other. Since the back is a two-beat diagonal gait in reverse, using one rein and then the other will tend to untrack one diagonal pair of legs at a time. Pulling straight back on both reins at one time usually results in resistance and no backward movement. Be satisfied with a shifting of body weight rearward, releasing after every such response. Eventually, the horse will respond by taking a few steps back.

In this back sequence, note that the left hind has the white pastern. The legs move in diagonal pairs. As I lift the reins and set up a light tremor on the lines), the horse moves the left hind and the right front back (Photo 7.23).

In the next set of steps), the right hind and left front move back (Photo 7.24). The horse should not be "pulled" back. At first, it is natural for a horse to raise his head a little when backing. Eventually, you want the horse to round into the back.

7.23

7.24

Note: Although it is very productive to canter a horse on the long lines, be sure the lines are a minimum of 35 feet long so they can go around the horse's body and still allow the horse to canter a 20-meter circle. Cantering in long lines is too advanced for a two-year-old but suitable for horses over that age.

When a horse becomes proficient at long reining, you can move the lessons to larger spaces, such as an arena. This will give you room for a much greater variety of maneuvers. On 20 feet of line, this horse is warming up (Photo 7.25).

From the trainer's perspective, you can see some interesting things: The horse is trotting up nicely in a rounded frame, with his poll the highest point of his neck, slightly bent to the inside (Photo 7.26). Notice that there is more tension on the inside line between the horse's mouth and the surcingle ring than there is between the surcingle ring and my hand. This shows the importance of finding a surcingle with ringsthat won't trap the lines! Notice that the outside line lies on top of the horse's hock where it should be, but the line is quite loose. I leave the outside line loose for a round, hoping that the horse will take the invitation and move his head slightly to the left, which would "unstick" the inside line. Ultimately, I stop the horse but find that the surcingle ring is upright and the line was not "stuck" anywhere. It was just a bit of friction and a reluctance of the horse to pull against that slight pressure!

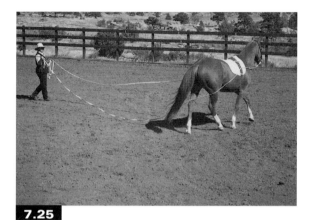

7.25

7.26

As your horse develops on the long line, insist on the same good frame he had in his longeing work. Here the horse is framed up well between the lines with an uphill topline, appropriate inside bend, and good impulsion (Photo 7.27).

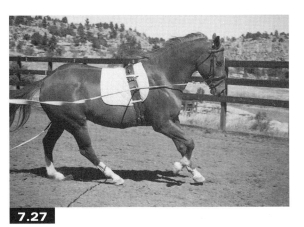

7.27

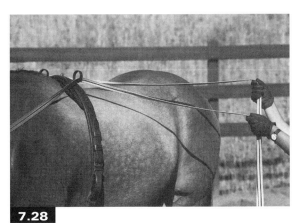

7.28

Because lines running through top terrets approximate the level of the rider's hands, you have the potential to work on advanced movements. The top terret position is particularly well suited to collected change of rein because the lines pass easily over the horse's back from one side to the other. When working on spirals, the top terret position allows you to preserve the horse's more collected frame. The top terret phase of driving is appropriate for developing a collected or "up-in-the-bridle" horse who typically travels with a high head carriage. The horse must be experienced and collected for this style of long lining to be productive (Photo 7.29). If the horse is not ready,

When you are ready to work on more close-up collected work, you can use the Danish style of long lining, in which the lines pass through the top terrets of the surcingle (Photo 7.28).

7.29

using the lines in such a high position could encourage him to hollow his neck, come above the bit, twirl, or rear.

Ground Driving the Western Horse

You can ground drive using the Western saddle. The lines through the stirrups have a low point of pull. This horse is ready for "plow driving" (Photo 7.30).

The stirrups are hobbled under the horse's belly, using a stirrup hobble strap. Note the large opening the Western stirrup provides for the long lines (Photo 7.31). Be aware that the lines can get caught between the stirrup and the stirrup leather.

7.31

If this happens often, you might need to wrap that junction with a cotton leg wrap or bandaging material.

The long lines can be snapped directly to the bit. But if you want to protect a nice bit, you can use a pair of water straps (from riding reins) as a go-between (Photo 7.32).

In this close-up of a water strap affixed to the bit with a quick-release knot made in the latigo string, the X in the center of the keeper is where the snap would be attached (Photo 7.33).

This four-year-old gelding patiently waits for last-minute adjustments. It takes time and some jostling to get the lines threaded through the stirrups, coiled up ready to use, and to give the cinch a last minute tightening (Photo 7.34). It's best if

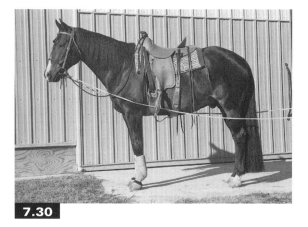

7.30

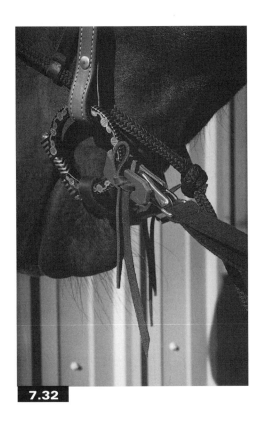

7.32

7.33

the horse has learned to stand patiently because it is difficult to do all of this and also hold onto the horse. The prior emphasis on "Whoa" pays off.

The sacking out to ropes and lines will show its worth the first time you draw the ropes over the horse's topline in preparation for first long lining (Photo 7.35).

Prevent anticipation, build even more patience, and give yourself an extra minute

7.34

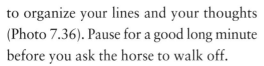

to organize your lines and your thoughts (Photo 7.36). Pause for a good long minute before you ask the horse to walk off.

Keep a safe distance behind and ask the horse to walk on (Photo 7.37). Asking for a gentle turn soon after you start off is a good idea because it lets the horse see you and will give you a better chance of controlling the horse if he bolts.

As the horse progresses, you will begin sending him out to the side to work around you in a circle. Early in the young horse's lessons, be sure to use lightweight

lines so the horse carries his head up and out, which is natural and desirable for a horse in this stage of training. The piece of pie configuration that is characteristic of longeing is evident when long lining as well (Photo 7.38).

Be aware that if your lines are too short or the horse is pulling into a larger circle, the outside line especially will get fairly snug and could cause the horse to counterflex. In spite of his energetic movement, and a quite tight outside line, this young horse is still bending his body into the

7.38

7.37

direction of movement in a respectable arc (Photo 7.39). I'd like him to not be leaning so much inward so I have tried to "hold" him up momentarily with the outside line. This will come in time.

Try to keep the outside line up above the hock because if it slips down, it can become hooked and get you into trouble. Here I am asking for a turn out of the circle at a trot (Photo 7.40). I'm taking with the right line, but since the line has slipped down, the action of the right line on the horse's mouth is governed more by the

7.39

7.40

7.41

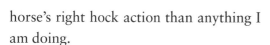

7.42

horse's right hock action than anything I am doing.

Stay well behind the horse's hindquarters as you drive him in a circle. This will help prevent the outside line from becoming tight and will allow the horse to move in a natural frame. I am facing the horse's hindquarters and the horse is caught between the lines nicely, rounding at a lope (Photo 7.41). He is stepping well under himself.

Whoops! If you get too far ahead of the horse, as indicated by the position of these lines and the horse's expression, you are inviting trouble (Photo 7.42). The horse's tendency here is to stop or turn. The more the left line is pulled to try to stop the horse, the more it turns him to the left in a tight curl. If he starts spinning around, you can end up with an official "spaghetti twirl."

Comments on a Typical Ground Driving Session

The horse starts out in the warm-up at a jog with little impulsion (Photo 7.43). His poll is low. He is coasting.

When I ask him to "Trot on," he starts increasing his impulsion as evidenced by a deeper reach with his hind leg (Photo 7.44). This automatically elevates his head, and his face line comes in front of the vertical a few degrees, both appropriate and desirable changes for the increase in impulsion. Note that his nose is tipped into the circle and his body shows signs of bending.

At the lope, he's a picture of roundness and collection with dropped croup, rounded back, and collected strides (Photo 7.45). His poll has dropped, and he's come a little behind the vertical in response to the increase of pressure on the inside line asking for bend.

Walking in the second direction, the horse shows signs of relaxation. He is reaching down and stretching, has a moist mouth, and is striding well under himself for a walk (Photo 7.46). Relaxation is necessary before asking for upward transitions in the second direction.

The lope to the right shows more correct form than Photo 7.45 to the left. Here he shows inside flexion, extreme reach

7.43

7.44

7.45

with the inside hind, and an elevated poll, all signs of a horse working in a collected and balanced frame (Photo 7.47). There is optimum tension on the lines for this style of ground driving.

Even when landing on the leading foreleg, which is the "lowest" point of the lope stride, the horse maintains the roundness and balance of the previous photo (Photo 7.48). If you find the horse dives down-

ward on the leading foreleg and loses his good form, you might want to go back to longeing with side reins.

Here is a rather abrupt "Whoa" from a lope (Photo 7.49). You can tell by the way the horse is squatting that he powered down in a hurry. This mainly came from a voice command, as evidenced by the slack outside line and just moderate tension on the inside line. But remember

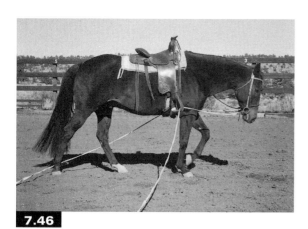

7.46

7.48

7.47

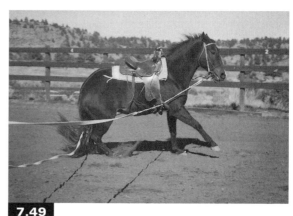

7.49

to be careful when using long lines—you have a lot of leverage between your hands and the bit in the horse's mouth.

When teaching a horse to turn, be sure that he is tracking forward with good impulsion (Photo 7.50). If you try to turn a horse who is already on the verge of stopping, he will die in the turn. Look for a moment when the horse's head position is lowered and relaxed. If you try

to turn a horse who has braced his back and locked his head, you will meet with resistance.

Lift up the rein for the goal direction, in this case the left rein for a turn left (Photo 7.51). At the same time, give with the right rein.

Maintain slightly more contact on the left line as you give with the right line (Photo 7.52). At this point the horse could

7.50

7.52

7.51

7.53

stall if you gave an accidental cue with the right line.

Take with the left and give with the right in appropriate amounts so the horse turns in the manner you desire (Photo 7.53). With a more advanced horse, you can maintain considerable contact on the outside line during the turn to ask for a slightly more collected turn.

When you move out to work in larger areas, don't forget the importance of "Whoa" as a means of controlling your horse and getting him to focus on the lesson at hand (Photo 7.54). Things can get out of control in a hurry, so the more certain you are of being able to stop your horse and have him stand when you want him to, the safer it will be for both you

7.54

7.56

7.55

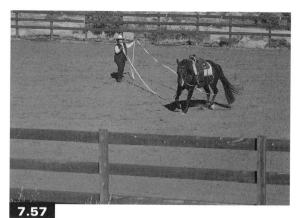

7.57

and your horse. Note that the horse is stopped directly on the track of the circle. I let the lines lie on the ground (which keeps the weight of the lines off the horse's mouth) while we both take a minute break. When work resumes, I will pick them up. If you don't sack a horse out to ropes all over his body, he will likely kick to be rid of the lines across his cannons and fetlocks.

In a turn on the hindquarters to the right, the horse crosses his left front over his right front (Photo 7.55).

In a change of rein out of the circle (outside turn) on long lines, the horse is on a serpentine pattern (Photo 7.56). I am just getting ready to walk forward quickly to keep up. It looks as though I'm ready to step on the ends of the long lines. Take care.

In a shallow-loop serpentine, I change the horse's bend every few strides. I walk a straight line forward as the horse makes a series of half circles at the trot (Photo 7.57).

A *rollback* is a lope, a set and turn, and a lope off in the opposite direction. In an early rollback sequence, the horse starts out loping on the right lead (Photo 7.58). I'm gathering lines so I can gather up slack quickly in the left line.

7.58

7.59

7.60

By taking with the left line and popping the horse on the right haunch with the right line, you make the horse change direction. During this rollback into the fence, the horse is not very collected during the "set," as evidenced by the spread of his legs (Photo 7.59). So that you don't accidentally bring the horse down to a trot, be sure to give him enough slack on the outside line for the sudden change of direction.

He manages to organize his hind legs, pushing off with both of them simultaneously as he lopes off on the left lead (Photo 7.60).

Here is a change of rein out of the circle that includes a flying change of lead. The horse is loping left lead and the flying change occurs on a straight line. From a lope left lead you can see the outside line already tightening (Photo 7.61).

The change has taken place, and the horse is now loping on the right lead (Photo 7.62).

When working obstacles such as ground poles, take care to approach the center of the obstacle (Photo 7.63).

Work alongside your horse on about 6 feet of line. This will give you enough room so that you don't have to walk through

7.61

7.62

the obstacle yourself, but can walk on the outside edge of the poles (Photo 7.64).

Similarly, with a bridge, line up the horse so his first step is dead center (Photo 7.65). Give the horse enough play in the lines so he can look down at the bridge and see where he is going to step.

7.63

7.65

7.64

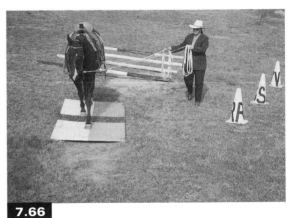

7.66

Once he's on the bridge, I drift behind the horse so I can turn him in a sharp left turn after the obstacle (Photo 7.66).

Cones provide a visual aid that can help you teach a horse bending. Set up the cones 3 to 4 feet apart. (These were set at 32 inches, which was kind of tight.) Use three to five cones. Walking a horse through closely spaced cones further hones the bending and change of direction lesson that you started in the arena as shallow serpentines. As soon as the horse passes the cone with his front legs, it is time to apply the aid for the turn (Photo 7.67).

7.67

7.68

7.69

This aid came a bit too late (Photo 7.68). The horse has already stepped "straight" past the optimum point to step to his right. I apply a bit more pressure on the right line cue to rescue the moment. This asks the horse to make a sharp turn.

He made it into the "hole" between the next cones (Photo 7.69).

Obstacle work is valuable for both the trainer and the horse because the goals and markers are definite and measurable.

7.70

When you are confident your horse is under control, you can further test him by long-lining out in the open, using bushes as obstacles for bending practice (photo 7.70).

Problems and Solutions

Many of the problems and their solutions that you might encounter while long lining are covered at the end of Chapter 6. Additional problems and solutions, specific to long lining are covered here.

PROBLEM   The "spaghetti twirl."

SOLUTION   The horse wraps himself up in the lines by turning and facing the trainer, becoming frightened, continuing to spin, and getting tangled in the lines. This can be a real setback, complete with friction burns, so avoid it at all costs. Thoroughly familiarize the horse with the equipment and use progressive stages of long lining styles. A sacked-out horse should stand and let you untangle him (Photo 7.71). Keep even contact on the lines, paying special attention to the inside line. Take care not to exert tense, unyielding pressure on it. Rather, use the inside line occasionally to push the horse

7.71

(with a pop to the hip) over to the outside line. Assert the driving aids (lines and voice) early.

PROBLEM   The horse gets the outside line under his tail and "reacts" (Photo 7.72).

SOLUTION   Don't pull on the outside line; keep it slack. Use your inside line to bring the horse into the circle, as if longeing. When the horse relaxes, his tail will unclamp and the line will drop. Review sacking out to ropes, as described earlier.

PROBLEM   The trainer drops a line. This can happen if the lines are too short, if the pen is too large, or if the handler is inexperienced. The horse's reaction to this may be inconsequential if he has been properly sacked out and knows "Whoa."

7.72

SOLUTION   The best thing to do is let the horse continue if you think you can reach down and pick up the line. If it is an outside line and it has moved too far away from you, use the inside line to bring the horse into the center of the circle and stop. If the inside line is dropped, take care not to pull on the outside line; otherwise, you may turn the horse to the outside of the circle since there is no inside line to counteract and keep him on the track. Ease the horse to a halt and gather up the lines.

PROBLEM   The trainer gets tangled in the lines.

SOLUTION   Some trainers prefer to carry the lines in a separate coil in each hand, others let the excess line trail behind them. The method of choice depends on how far away the horse is working from you, how much line is left over, and what you are most comfortable with. Getting a hand or a foot tangled in a loop is certainly dangerous! Stop the horse immediately but calmly. Don't panic, or the horse might panic and make things much worse. Carry a pocketknife at all times and know how to use it.

PROBLEM   The horse overflexes and gets behind the bit.

SOLUTION   The lines may be too heavy, the trainer's hands too heavy, the bit too severe, or not enough impulsion is being generated. Evaluate these things and make corrections. You want the horse to be light!

Epilogue

Never has the phrase "champing at the bit" had greater meaning for me than this past winter. While I have been putting the finishing touches on this book and *101 Longeing and Long Lining Exercises: English and Western,* my nine horses have enjoyed a two-month holiday, complete with pasture turn-out and time to just be horses. But spring is here and I'm just about to head out the door for an intensive eight months of horse training. Besides my riding horses, I have a yearling, a two-year-old, a three-year-old, and two four-year-olds, so there will be plenty of groundwork and goal setting going on. I am anxious to help these young horses reach their maximum potential and become good working partners. I hope this book and its companion volume inspire and help you to do the same with your horses.

Recommended Reading

German National Equestrian Federation. *Lungeing*. Addington, Buckingham: Kenilworth Press, 1990.

Harris, Susan E. *The USPC Guide to Longeing and Ground Training*. New York: Howell Book House, 1997.

_____. *The USPC Manual of Horsemanship, Intermediate Horsemanship*. New York: Howell Book House, 1995.

Hill, Cherry. *101 Arena Exercises, A Ringside Guide for Horse and Rider*. Pownal, VT: Storey Publishing, 1995.

_____. *101 Longeing and Long Lining Exercises: English and Western*. New York: Howell Book House, 1998.

_____. *Becoming an Effective Rider, Developing Your Mind and Body for Balance and Unity*. Pownal, VT: Garden Way, 1991.

_____. *The Formative Years, Raising and Training the Horse from Birth to Two Years*. Ossining, NY: Breakthrough, 1988.

_____. *Horse Handling and Grooming*. Pownal, VT: Storey Publishing, 1997.

_____. *Horse Health Care*. Pownal, VT: Storey Publishing, 1997.

_____. *Horsekeeping on a Small Acreage, Facilities Design and Management*. Pownal, VT: Garden Way, 1990.

_____. *Making Not Breaking, The First Year Under Saddle.* Ossining, NY: Breakthrough, 1992.

Hill, Cherry, and Richard Klimesh, CJF. *Maximum Hoof Power: How to Improve Your Horse's Performance Through Proper Hoof Management.* New York: Howell Book House, 1994.

Inderwick, Sheila. *Lungeing The Horse & Rider.* Devon: David & Charles, 1977.

Loriston-Clarke, Jennie. *Lungeing and Long-Reining.* Addington, Buckingham: Kenilworth Press, 1993.

Sivewright, Molly. *Lessons on the Lunge for Horse and Rider.* London: Ward Lock, 1996.

Stashak, Ted, DVM, and Cherry Hill. *Horseowner's Guide to Lameness.* Philadelphia: Williams & Wilkins, 1995.

Manufacturers that distribute to tack shops and catalogs nationwide:

Les Vogt's Equiline	1279 W. Stowell, Unit H Santa Maria, CA 93454 Phone 1-888-LES-VOGT (Snaffle bits)
Pro Equine Division of Farnam	P.O. Box 34820 Phoenix, AZ 85067-4820 Phone 1-800-327-9792 (Protective leg boots)
Top Tack, Inc.	802 Hillman Rd. Yakima, WA 98908 Phone 1-800-419-1392 (Manufacturer of specialized tack for longeing and long lining)
Topline Horse Gear	P.O. Box 1779 Jacksonville, OR 97530 Phone 1-514-899-3994 (Manufacturer of longeing and long lining equipment)

Index